DIVORCE AND
REMARRIAGE

*Divorced Christians
Can Get Remarried*

Sheila Sims

First published by Dog Ear Publishing
4010 W. 86th Street, Ste H
Indianapolis, IN 46268
www.dogearpublishing.net

dog ear
<u>PUBLISHING</u>

ISBN: 978-160844-397-0

This book is printed on acid-free paper.

Printed in the United States of America

Table of Contents

ADULTERY

FAMILY PROBLEMS

THE REAL REASON FOR HAVING CHILDREN

THE REAL PURPOSE FOR MARRIAGE

THE REAL PURPOSE FOR MONEY

PRAYER

FAITH

CHOOSING TO REMAIN SINGLE

Dedication

This book is dedicated to my handsome husband of over twenty years, **TIMOTHY B. SIMS, SR.,** who made a big sacrifice by allowing me to stay home and write. Thank you sweetheart for loving me, motivating me, and inspiring me. I appreciate everything you've done for me and the children.

I also dedicate this book to my six children (my friends) whom I love with all of my heart: **David, Latoya, Keirri, Diana, Timmy, and Christopher.**

I would also like to thank **Mrs. Patsy Talbert,** my wonderful mother and friend. Thank you MOM for always listening and believing in me.

I would like to say "Thank You" to my beloved friend who is a woman after God's own heart, **MRS. CELESTE GRIMES.** God used you to be my cheerleader, my motivator, and my supporter for years.

I would like to thank my entire family for their patience and understanding while this book was being written.

About the Author

Sheila Sims is a happily remarried Christian businesswoman.

The author is a college graduate, and a Phi Theta Kappa Honor Society member, and a mother of six. She attended Bible School, and is a former Sunday School teacher.

While married to her best friend in the whole world, she began working at Sidley & Austin, a prestigious law firm in New York City. This is the same law firm where President, Barack Obama (America's First African American President) and his wife, Michelle, were both attorneys at Sidley & Austin's Chicago office.

She has been trained to *walk by faith, and not by sight* by some of the greatest and most successful pastors and teachers. She believes that faith is obeying God's written and spoken word. And she knows the importance of following His instructions. For instance, she recalls a time when she was led by the Holy Spirit to change her career in Corporate America for a more rewarding job, and that was to become a home-school mom, an author, and a wife of twenty years.

Introduction

God Answered My Prayer

I became a Christian at the age of twelve, and I couldn't seem to put my Bible down. Therefore, I became a walking, talking Bible. That's when everything changed. My mother remarried, and we moved into a beautiful house in Queens, NY. There was no more fighting between her and my father; there was only peace.

God Said, No!
But I Married Him Anyway

While standing at the alter I heard God say, "No!" I knew by His voice, that I shouldn't disobey. It was obvious that this marriage wasn't for me. But the guests were there, and I didn't want to disappoint them. I breathed a prayer, promising God that I would annul the marriage the next day. Then satan began telling me, "You're 19, you don't want to go back home!" So I stayed, and took a chance, hoping I could change him.

At that time, I attended a church where we didn't practice divorce or birth control. So I remained in an unequally-yoked marriage for almost ten years. Four children were born, and it was hard and scary. That's when I began to understand that the marriage wasn't the Will of God.

A Decision to be Free

I would have gotten divorced sooner, if only I hadn't been taught, "Getting divorced means to remain alone for the rest of my life." I needed a husband, and my children needed a father.

Ten years later, I'd had enough. My children were precious to me, and I wouldn't tolerate the abuse that comes with the use of drugs and alcohol. Sexual immorality was the reason a man could divorce his wife, but what did the Bible say about divorcing a husband?

Next, I decided to give myself the gift of being free from the constant pain of betrayal and rejection. And the only way I could be truly free from this man, was to let him go–so I filed for divorce.

Getting Remarried

After my divorce, I prayed and asked God not to let my children grow up without a father. And although I was prepared to live alone for the rest of my life, as time went by, the loneliness became unbearable. And I prayed...

> Father, in the name of Jesus, please help me! You said that I'm not suppose to commit fornication, and I don't want to. But I can't take feeling like this anymore. So please send me a friend until you bless me with a husband, because I'm very lonely.

And He did! **At the lowest point in my life, the Holy Spirit led me to talk to my girlfriend's brother, who later became my husband. And we have been happily married for more than twenty years.**

While married to my best friend in the whole world, I was able to finish college, and soon began working at Sidley & Austin, a prestigious law firm in New York City. During the time I worked there, Barack Obama (America's first African American President) and his wife, Michelle, were both attorneys at Sidley & Austin's Chicago office.

Getting My Tubes Untied

After we were married, we were faced with a major problem. He was 32 years old, and he didn't have any children. And I had gotten my tubes tied after the birth of my fourth child. I was terrified when he asked me to have a baby because I already had four children. All kinds of frightening thoughts raced through my mind, "...what if he leaves me? Then I'll have five children to raise alone!"

But after we prayed, I was led to have an operation at Queens General Hospital in New York. And after one year of fertility testing, and six hours of microsurgery, my tubes were put back together. Ten months later I was pregnant with my fifth child. Then a year and seven months later, I gave birth to our second son. And of course, I had my tubes tied again.

Feeling Guilty
About Being Happy

Although I was happily re-married, I could still hear my ex-pastor's voice speaking against *Divorce and Remarriage*. Every time I heard it, I felt depressed. I told myself, over and over again, that if it wasn't God's will for me to be remarried, then I wouldn't be so happy. But the nagging in my head continued.

I have been remarried for over twenty years, and I've been called by God to write "Divorce and Remarriage" to answer questions Christians have about this topic. This will erase the pain people have about remarriage.

God said, "Write the Book!"

While working at the law firm, the Lord impressed upon me that there was something He wanted me to do. The realization was so overwhelming that

I thought, "My goodness, God wants me to do something Great! What could it be?" And the Holy Spirit answered and said, "Write the book." (I was to research the scriptures, and write the revelations that were given to me). Other topics I wrote about was: God's purpose for marriage, and His purpose for having children. Raising step-children with your own. Protecting our children from gang involvement. And what to do about family problems.

After my research I discovered that *divorce and remarriage* is one of the ways in which God delivers His people from their past sins, and from the mistake of marrying the wrong person. This book is absolutely clear on the fact that getting divorced (in order to marry another person) is called adultery. But for those who have made the mistake of committing adultery, it seems that forgiveness is available because they have not committed the unpardonable sin.

After years of researching the scriptures, I discovered that divorce and remarriage is God's Will; and I was set free.

Avoiding Divorce

The only way to avoid divorce is to ask God what to do, and then obey His instructions.

Who Should Read This Book

This book is highly recommended to those Christians who were taught that if they got divorced, they had to remain single for the rest of their lives. And for those Christians who have gotten remarried, but are still experiencing guilt or pain.

Afraid of being talked about, left out, and going to hell, many divorced Christians sadly chose to remain alone for years.

The truth is that the blood of Jesus has cleansed you from all premeditated and past sins, and from all mistakes committed through ignorance or disobedience.

This means that Jesus died so you wouldn't have to suffer the consequences of your sins for the rest of your life.

Reasons People Get Divorced

Adultery is not the only reason people get divorced. They get divorced over things that most people never think about:

What if a spouse is sentenced to 5 or 10 years (or **life in prison**).

Or gets a **sex change** operation. Is this grounds for a divorce.

Or is **missing in military action**.

What if **adultery** was a mistake, but the innocent spouse refuses to forgive.

In an abusive relationship, how much **abuse** should the spouse take.

In **a violent situation**, should the couple separate, and for how long.

If a Christian has been **divorced and remarried twice**, can that person get remarried a third time?

What if a person got divorced before he (or she) became a Christian. And today, their ex-spouse is with someone else.

Should a Christian pray for reconciliation?
Or wait until their ex-spouse dies before he (or she) can get married again?

In this book, **you will learn how to stay married,** but if a divorce can't be avoided, you'll know exactly what the Bible says.

Divorce and Remarriage is Biblical and Legal

Many believe that divorce and remarriage is not biblical or legal. But after examining the scriptures, you will see for yourself that God's will is for His divorced children to have happy remarried lives.

**For the Lord has called you
...a woman forsaken and grieved in spirit,
...a wife forsaken from her youth,**

...but with my great mercies I will gather you.

**...with my Everlasting Kindness
I will have mercy on you,
says the Lord, your Saviour.**

Isaiah 54:6-8 LMSA

DIVORCE

Should Christians Get Divorced?

While Jesus was teaching, the Pharisees came to test Him by asking, "Is it Legal for a man to Divorce his wife?" They were really asking Jesus, **"Has God changed His mind about allowing us to get divorced?"**

(Mark 10:2)

Jesus asked them, "What did Moses command you?" They said, "Moses permitted a man to write *A Certificate of Divorce* and to send her away."

Jesus explained, that Moses wrote this law because the people were sinning against God. So God made divorce **legal**. This way, no one was breaking His laws. Jesus further explained, that from the beginning, men didn't divorce their wives. For example:

> Adam and Noah didn't. Abraham, Isaac, and Jacob didn't. Neither did Joseph or Moses.

There was no need to get divorced, because God doesn't make mistakes. Therefore, those who are married according to **"The Perfect Will of God"** must not separate. But since they do, let's discuss their reasons—and whether they're biblical.

The Reasons People Get Divorced

If one spouse refuses to commit to the marriage, then at some point divorce will become an issue that will fall under one of these categories:

ADULTERY, SEPARATION, or IRRECONCILABLE DIFFERENCES.

Abandonment (Leaving home with no intention of returning)

Unintentional
Abandonment (Missing in war, or being sentenced to life in prison)

Abuse   (Physical violence, verbal and mental abuse, drug and alcohol addiction)

Adultery   (Having sex with someone else, child abuse, incest, homosexuality)

Infidelity   (Being entertained by strippers, phone sex, and internet pornography)

Neglect   (Withholding sex, affection, and attention)

Rejection   (To completely ignore, or to show no interest)

The Reasons Divorce is Allowed in the New Testament

Divorce is allowed in the New Testament if the husband or wife commits adultery. However, Christians are still responsible for asking God for wisdom before filing for a divorce.

There are times when the Lord will permit a divorce. Particularly when the adulterous spouse has decided to continue in adultery.

On the other hand, He might lead the innocent spouse to forgive the adultery. Especially if it was a regretful mistake. God knows when a person has truly repented, and has abandoned all wrong doing.

Our job is to trust Him as He leads us by His Holy Spirit. We do this by following peace. For instance, if God tells you to forgive, and you refuse, then you wont have any peace. But once you forgive, your peace will return.

This scripture reveals two reasons for New Testament divorces:

> *But if the unbelieving **depart**, let him depart.*
> *A brother or **a sister** is not under **bondage** IN SUCH CASES; but*
> *God has called us to **peace**.*
>
> *1 Cor. 7:15*

DEPART   To abandon, to leave, to go away, to desert, die,
means: withdraw, forsake, vacate, quit, retreat, exit.

BONDAGE   Slavery, misery, sorrow, pain and oppression.
means: **A continual state of frustration and stress.** Bound,
              restrained.

PEACE   Living and working together **without (continual)**
means: strife, arguing, and fighting. Getting along, friend-
              ship, harmony.

The Reasons Divorce isn't Allowed
in the New Testament

Jesus taught his disciples that divorce is not used for terminating one relationship—in order to begin a new one.

> *And I say unto you, Whosoever shall put away his wife,*
> *except it be for fornication,*
> ***and shall marry another**, (girlfriend he's been seeing)*
> *committeth adultery:*
>
> *and whoso (a man in love with a married woman)*
> ***marrieth her which is put away** (divorced for having sex with him)*
> *doth commit adultery.*
>
> *Mat. 19:9*

And if a woman divorces her husband
and marries another man *(the boyfriend she's been seeing)*
she commits adultery.

Mark 10:12

The Reasons Divorce was Allowed
in the Old Testament

I gave faithless Israel her certificate of divorce
and sent her away because of all her adulteries.

Jer. 3:8 NIV

When Israel worshiped other gods made of wood and stone, God called it **adultery**. He divorced Israel for her unfaithfulness to Him.

...Return, faithless Israel declares the Lord,
*I will frown on you no longer, for **I am merciful**...*
I will not be angry forever.

Jer. 3:12 NIV

Even God doesn't stay angry forever!

The Reasons Divorce Wasn't Allowed
in the Old Testament

*If a man finds a damsel who is a virgin who is not engaged, and takes her, **and [has sex] with her**, and they are found; Then the man who slept with her shall give to the damsel's father fifty shekels of silver, and she shall be his wife; because he has humbled her, and **he has no right to divorce her**.*

Duet. 22:28-29

God told Moses that when a man had sex with an (unmarried) virgin, once the matter was discovered, he must pay her father, then marry her, and loose all his rights to divorce her.

Here's another reason:

> *If any man take a wife, and go in unto her, and **then hate her**...*
> *Duet. 22:13-21 LMSA*

Divorce wasn't allowed when a man took a wife, had sex with her, didn't like it, and would lie to her father about her not being a virgin. Fortunately, it was their custom to save the blood-stained bed sheets from the wedding night. This item was given to the father the next day as proof that his daughter was a virgin. If necessary, the father would take this sheet to the Elders, and the consequences for bringing an evil report of whoredom upon the good name of the woman would be a beating, a fine, and the lost of all rights to (ever) divorce her.

No Choice, But to Divorce

Sinners don't know God when they get married. So they have no power to keep their marital promises. Although unbelievers would like God to protect their relationships, they have no legal right to expect Him to, because they have no "Covenant" with Him. Consequently, many of their marriages end in divorce.

Christian marriages depend heavily upon the Word of God and the power of His Holy Spirit. But if God isn't put first, then the relationship is subject to end in divorce. If this happens, then both have a responsibility to talk to God (not run away from Him). He loves His children, and will put their lives back together.

Unequally Yoked

To avoid grief, heartache (and in some cases) to avoid children growing up without both parents, God clearly commands us not to be **unequally yoked** (2 Cor. 6:14). Unfortunately, some **Christians consistently remarry unbelievers**, only to find themselves divorced again and again.

(Duet. 24:1-4)

Satan Arranges Marriages, too!

Christians aren't aware that **some** unsaved people **have been assigned by satan to marry believers.** The purpose is **to drive them crazy,** get them hooked on drugs, provoke them to commit child abuse, and lead them to early graves. Sadly, unbelievers aren't aware that the enemy is using them to make the believer's life a living nightmare.

Self-Righteous Marriages

Some Christians, either unaware of the scriptures, or for some reason, **marry *"self-righteous people"*** who have no interest in going to church. These are good people with godly morals, but they're not interested in pleasing God. As a result, these dear sweet (unsaved) people are **powerless against unclean spirits that are assigned to destroy the marriage.**

You're Called to Repair
or Restore Something

For we (including you) are his workmanship,
created *in Christ Jesus unto*
GOOD WORKS,
which God hath before ordained (or planned)
that we should WALK IN THEM.

Eph. 2:10

God has assigned every Christian to repair, or to restore something. These are the good works we've been called to do. But in order to fulfill our assignments, we have to walk in obedience to the *"written"* and the *"spoken"* Word.

Perhaps you've gone to church for years, paid tithes, and love God; but there are dreams and visions inside of you that you desperately want to accomplish, but you don't know how. If you've tried everything and nothing seems to work, prepare yourself, I'm about to tell you some good news.

You're at the point in your life where you want to know the truth. Once you ask God to show you the truth, He's going to direct you to a place where you will be taught how to have strong faith. The church you're attending has taught you foundational truths about living Holy. In fact, you have a Master's Degree in Living Holy. Now, you want to grow to another level.

You Know that God's Word is the Truth

You're a Christian because you believe that **precious blood was poured out** to wash away your sins. And you know that God's Word is the truth because in the Old Testament, the prophets accurately foretold the birth, death, and resurrection of Jesus Christ

(Luke 24:27).

Once you've decided that God's Word is the truth, then you'll begin seeking God, instead of human wisdom. And no matter what **the Spirit of God** tells you to do, you're willing to do it, because your survival depends upon getting good results.

In the past, **when you heard the Spirit of God speaking to you**, His commands were ignored because it sounded to good to be true, or perhaps you thought He was making suggestions. But you didn't know that the still small voice was the answer to your prayers.

If God wasn't listening to us, then why would He tell us to pray. You see, we have to recognize when God is speaking to us.

Decide to Obey His Voice

When life becomes serious, and you decide to obey the voice of God, this is when you'll begin to grow up spiritually. And when you attend the Bible study He leads you to, the teaching may include some of your favorite scriptures, but once you begin to examine the scriptures closely, **God will**

open up your understanding. Then you'll discover truths you never knew before, and that's when you'll begin walking in agreement with God's Word.

Then **you'll start receiving results in those barren areas of your life**. And yes, this is where the **persecution will begin**. People will try to talk you out of it, you'll be criticized, laughed at, and even rejected by people you care about. But remember what the Lord Jesus said in Mark 10:29-30.

> *Verily I say unto you, there is no man that **has left** house,*
> *or brother, or sisters, or father, or mother, or children,*
> *or lands, **for my sake, and the gospel's,***
> *But he shall receive an hundredfold now in this time, [in] houses,*
> *and Brothers, and sisters, and mothers...*
> *with persecutions. And in the world to come eternal life.*

When you're ready to know the truth, God will make the truth available to you. Once **your knowledge increases** and you start walking in Agreement with God's Word (and begin experiencing results) at that point, you'll be willing to leave *brothers, sisters, father, mother* (and all traditions, and **doctrines of men**)... *for the Gospel.*

If you're willing to give up traditions, doctrines, legalism and rules made by men, and start living in Agreement with God's Word, you'll receive in this life **all** that you desire, and in the life to come—eternal life.

No More Filthy Rags

It's sad the way some Christians have been taught that God sees their **righteousness** as filthy rags. First of all, **this does not apply to Christians.** In Isa. 64:6, Israel sinned, and God described their unrighteousness as *Filthy rags*.

This incorrect teaching is the reason why many Christians feel unclean, and think they're unworthy of the blessings of God.

For he hath made him to be sin for us
who knew no sin; that we might
be made the righteousness of God *in him.*

2 Cor. 5:21

If God has made us righteous, how can our righteousness be as filthy rags?

The blood of Jesus washed you clean, **threw out the filthy rags**, and put you in right-standing with God. Don't allow anyone to put those filthy rags back on you. God wants you to have a powerful self-image of yourself dressed in purple and gold silk. Look at what He said:

I clothed you with embroidered cloth ...and leather shoes.
I decked you *also with ornaments and I put* ***bracelets*** *on your arms, and* ***a chain*** *on your neck.*

*And I put ...****earrings*** *in your ears and a beautiful* ***crown*** *upon your head. Thus you were decked with* ***gold*** *and* ***silver*** *and your clothes were of fine linen and* ***silk.***

You ate fine flour, and honey, and oil. And ***you were*** ***exceedingly beautiful,*** *and* ***you prospered*** *into a royal nation. And your beauty was perfect ...which* ***I had put upon you,*** ***saith the Lord God.***

Ezek.16:10-14

God did not allow His son to die in our place (on the cross) so we could walk around dressed in filthy rags.

Jesus Christ, also known as **the Last Adam** (1 Cor. 15:45) came to undo what the first Adam did. Both men were created by God. The first one disobeyed, so **God had to send another one**, and this one (Jesus) OBEYED. As a result of Jesus' obedience, God **forgave** the sin Adam committed, and **removed the curse Adam caused** (Gal. 3:13). Now, we stand before a Holy God who sees us as sinless, righteous, and reconciled (Col. 1:20). **We're no longer judged by Adam's sin,** we don't even think like him anymore.

You're In A Position of Power

You've been reconciled to God! This means that **God paid satan a lot for you**. And once you became His, your spirit was restored to a position of right-standing with Him. Then He sat you on a throne right next to Him, and immediately you were reconnected to your rightful position of power, and control over the Earth (Rev. 5:10). A position of prestige and influence. A position of preferential treatment!

> *And Jesus came and spake unto them, saying,*
> *All power [authority or **privilege**]*
> *is given unto me in heaven and **in earth**.*
>
> *Mat. 28:18*

Since you're no longer judged by Adam's sin, the question is, who are you now? You're now identified with Christ (the second Adam):

> *And He raised us up **together** with Him*
> *and made us sit down **together**...*
> *in the heavenly sphere... in Christ Jesus.*
>
> *Eph. 2:6 AMP*

God raised Jesus from the dead, and made you sit with Christ at His own right hand. This is how you were restored to a position of power. **Now, let's see who you are:**

> *And [God] hath put all things under his [Jesus] feet,*
> *and gave him to be the **head** over all things to the church,*
> *which is his **body**...*
>
> *Eph. 1:22-23*

Jesus is the head, right? Well doesn't a head need a body? Of course it does, and **we're the body**. So if the head has all of the power and privileges in heaven and in Earth, then **the body must have those same privileges**, right? And who is the body of Christ? You and me, and the entire church.

And since all things have been put under Jesus' feet, then where is His feet? They're attached to His body–and the church is the body of Christ.

So what has God placed under your feet? Everything! He did this when He raised Jesus, who is (*the head*) of the church, to sit at His own right hand. But you can't have a head sitting on a throne next to God without a body, so God also raised up Jesus' body which is (*the church*).

Therefore, you are seated with Jesus far above demonic spirits, unfair rulers, people who try to dominate you, and everything that has a name; including poverty, sickness, unemployment, and divorce.

Nothing in this world is suppose to defeat you, just like nothing will defeat you in the New Heaven and Earth.

(Rev. 21 :1-2)

When Jesus ascended and left you here, **you inherited the privilege to (greatly benefit) from the Earth.** You have the Holy Spirit as a teacher to guide you to treasures of darkness, and hidden riches in secret places (Isa. 45:2-3). That's why Jesus sent the Holy Spirit to the Earth. His job is to teach us how to live in the Kingdom of God, and how to rule victoriously on the Earth. But you must listen to His voice, and obey Him.

Without Faith, it's Impossible
to Please God

Somebody taught you everything you believe concerning **divorce and remarriage.** But you wont have confidence to remarry unless you hear God's Word taught correctly. And after you hear the truth, the Word of God will become your reality, and you'll look forward to getting remarried.

Nothing is Impossible to Him that believe.

When you read something in the Bible, but you don't do what it says, it doesn't mean that you don't love God. It simply means that you don't understand the benefits of obeying His voice.

God is a Spirit whom you cannot see or touch, but you can hear Him, and He can hear you!

Ask God for A Confirmation

Jesus said, *My sheep hear my voice...*

God always answer your prayers. He always tell you how to get what you want. But you wont receive anything from Him until you follow His instructions.

Once you've received instructions through prayer, **if you don't agree with God**, then you'll be acting on your own, and you'll be responsible for the outcome.

If you're not sure if God was speaking to you (perhaps it was your own thoughts you heard) then you should ask Him to tell you again, or to make it clear. This is called a *confirmation*.

God will confirm His Word by giving you a scripture, or a dream, or a vision. You might receive a revelation or an inspiration in your heart. Or He might confirm His Word through a true prophet. It's always good to remember that **the prophet is not God**. And a prophecy only confirms what you already know in your heart. So once you're sure that it was God, courageously act on it.

Authority to Avoid Divorce

You have authority to avoid divorce, by obeying the Word of God, and fol-lowing the leading of the Holy Spirit.

When you ask God for help, you must expect something good to happen if you follow His instructions. So if He brings a scripture to your mind, with-out hesitation, you must be willing to find it, read it, and accept it as the truth. Or, if **He gives you a strategy for handling the situation**, you must be willing to obey it (by doing it). Look at my version of Isa. 1:19.

*You must be **willing to obey God**, in order*
to enjoy the good things in this land.

Remember, when Peter wanted to walk on water, he had to believe like a little child. So **he did exactly what Jesus told him to do,** he got out of the boat, and by doing so, he experienced the joy of walking on water.

The Choice is God's

But from the beginning of the creation,
*God made them **male and female**,*
*for this cause shall a man **leave his father and mother**,*
and cleave (BE JOINED) to his wife;
*and they two shall be — **one flesh**:*
*so they (ARE NO MORE TWO), but **one flesh**.*
*What therefore **(GOD HAS JOINED)** together,*
***let (NO MAN) separate**.*

Mark 10:6-9

Christians marry after receiving *"rhema"* which is the spoken Word of God. As confirmation, they might have received *"a logos"* from the written Word of God. This means that God selected and assigned them to each other for His own specific plans and purpose.

Before marriage, you might have an idea of what your mate should look like, but the choice is God's. If you disagree with God's choice, then how can you be sure you've got the right person?

When God Puts Two People Together

Can you remember making a decision in the past without God? Are you still dealing with the effects of that decision, although it was a long time ago? Well, divorcing without the wisdom of God will bring the same consequences!

When you know God has put the two of you together (when you've received rhema regarding your marriage) you must seek the wise counsel of God before removing what God has placed in order.

Mark 10:9

Your marriage is an assignment, given to you by God. And to ensure that the marriage is successful, He has provided wisdom:

> *For the Lord gives wisdom and from his mouth*
> *comes knowledge and understanding.*

Prov. 2:6 NIV

If you're having difficulty with something, God says to *"Seek first the Kingdom of God."* **This means to ask Him first, before asking anyone else.**

After receiving instructions, **if you have doubts**, search the scriptures to find out God's Will concerning your needs. After receiving a confirmation, if you believe that He's told you the truth, then follow His instructions, and expect results.

When God joins two people together, they become His handiwork. They're joined together to accomplish His will. If one of them decides to separate, the final decision (to divorce) should come from God—and God alone!

So don't be deceived by temporary sexual adventures, or illegal financial gain. It can cost everything you have: your family, your wealth, your health, your anointing, your relationship with God, and finally—eternal life.

Q.   Does the author of this book believe in people getting divorced:

A.   I don't believe in Christians getting divorced, instead I believe that Christians should obey the voice of the Holy Spirit and follow His instructions. As a result, God will fix their marriages.

But I also know that there are reasons some Christians can't avoid getting divorced, and they are left feeling lonely, confused, and trapped. They want to please God, but they don't know what to do.

In this book, I strongly advise each person to pray for their spouse, and seek the wise counsel of God, and to be led by His Spirit.

This book was written to set free those who are trapped in abusive marriages, and for those who believe that after they're divorced, they have to remain single (and childless) for the rest of their lives.

Although we're taught to avoid getting divorced, there are times when it can't be avoided. And along with divorce comes guilt, shame, fear, hopelessness, desperation, financial difficulties, celibacy, emotional problems, and loneliness. And each of these problems will be solved based on what each person believes.

So many Christians are living alone because they've been taught that getting remarried is a sin. –And it's not! **These lonely saints just want to be happy and have children, but they believe that God will send them to hell.**

This book has been written to give each person a complete understanding of "God's Will" concerning divorce and remarriage.

> ...*this is the confidence that we have in him,*
> *that, if we **ask any thing***
> ***according to his will** (which is "His Word")*
> *he hears us;*
> *And if **we know that he hear us**...*
> ***we know that we have the petitions** that we desired of him.*
> *1 John 5:14, 15*

This scripture tells us that God hears us when we pray *(His Will)*.
And since we know that *(His Will)* is His Word–then we don't have to make up prayers, instead we can pray the actual scriptures.

Q. **In Malachi 2:16, God said that He hates divorce, so how can you say that Christians can get divorced?**

A. Malachi 2:16 says:

> *For the Lord God of Israel says, " I hate divorce."*

But God never said that they couldn't get divorced. Instead,
in Deut. 24:1-4 says:

> *When a man takes a wife and marries her, and it happens
> that she find no favor in his eyes because he has found some
> uncleanness (indecency) in her, and he writes her **a certificate
> of divorce**, puts it in her hand, and sends her out of his house,
> when she has departed from his house,*
>
> *...and goes and **becomes another man's wife**,*
>
> *...if the last husband ...**divorces her**, or dies*
>
> *...then her former (first) husband who divorced her
>   must not take her back to be his wife...*

But God never said not to get divorced. Instead, in the New Testament
Jesus repeated Deut 24:1...

> *...it has been said, "whoever divorces his wife,
>   let him give her a certificate of divorce*
>
> *But I say to you that whoever divorces his wife for **any reason**
> except sexual immorality causes her to commit adultery...*
>   *Mat. 5:32*

The Reason God Hates Divorce

> *And did not God make (you and your wife) one (flesh)?
> Did not One make you and preserve your spirit alive?
> And **why (did God make you two) one?**
> Because **He sought a godly offspring** (Christian children)*
>
> *...Therefore take heed to yourselves, and
> **let no one deal treacherously—**
> and be faithless **to the wife of his youth.***
>   *Mal. 2:15 AMP*

God put you and your spouse together to do a job. That job is to serve Him, and it might include raising Godly children.

Your children are His (future) generation on the earth. However, **divorce threatens the future of the church.** Therefore, God warned, "Let no one deal treacherously and be unfaithful to the wife of his youth, because **"I hate DIVORCE, I hate SEPARATION, and I hate DOMESTIC VIOLENCE!"**

> *For I have chosen him [Abraham],*
> *so that **he will direct his children** and **his household** after him*
> *to keep the way of the Lord*
> *by doing what is right and just,*
> *so that **the Lord will bring** about for Abraham*
> ***what he has promised** him.*
>
> *Gen. 18:19 NIV*

God carefully selects two people to join in marriage. He chose Abraham because He knew that Abraham would teach his children and his entire household to expect God to do what He promised. Just like Abraham, you have to trust God's intelligence, and go to Him in prayer with whatever grievances you have against your spouse.

Complications of the Worst Kind

God knew that you and your spouse would make excellent parents, that's why He put you together. **But, when one leaves and refuses to obey the will of God (because he or she wants to marry another person) complications of the worst kind can happen.**

God's future generation is in danger of being lost whenever Christians become angry with Him.

No longer trusting God, the wounded spouse (and children) might **backslide**. Even worse, an instability storm might begin, as the offended spouse has stress levels reaching insurmountable proportions. Consumed by **rage** and **hatred**, tidal waves of repressed **anger** might overwhelm other family members.

Broken-hearted and overwhelmed by **grief**, those left behind could suffer from **mental illness** or **depression.** Lowered immune systems might leave them exposed to **colds, sickness,** or **other diseases**.

Overwhelmed by financial and time shortages, the (new) single parent may not want to **raise the children alone**.

Disenchanted with God, the children might become **promiscuous**, and seek love anywhere. Gangs are always on the look-out for kids who are neglected, unwanted, and whose parents don't have time for them. And once they join a gang, you can expect **violence, guns, sex, and drugs.**

The girls might think:

> *"My mom committed adultery, so why can't I have an abortion if I make a mistake and get pregnant."*

The boys might think:

> *"My father committed adultery, so why can't I smoke weed or sell **drugs...** or drink alcohol? And why should I raise some kid that probably isn't mine?"*

Beloved, please realize that divorce can destroy happy, Godly children.

Also, the new partner of the adulterous mate will never be completely secure in a relationship sown in treachery.

Living God's way is the only way men and women will ever be truly happy.

Search the Word of God and be led by His Holy Spirit. Don't divorce the wife (or husband) of your youth—without first seeking the wise counsel of God.

Divorce Affects Your Financial Blessings

In the Old Testament, women cried on the altar because their husbands had divorced them. God saw their tears, and heard their cries, and then He spoke against their husbands:

> *And this you do with double guilt;*
> ***you cover the altar*** *of the Lord with tears*
> *(shed by your unoffending wives, divorced by you*
> *that you might take heathen wives),*

As you can see, the altar was covered with the tears of the innocent spouse, **but the adulterous spouse's tears covered the altar too.** Why? Because God would not accept their offerings with favor any more.

> *and* ***with (your own) weeping and crying out***
> ***because the Lord does not regard your offering any more***
> ***or accept it with favor*** *at your hand.*
> *Yet you ask,* ***Why does He reject it?***

These women needed their husbands. They had sexual needs, and they had children to raise. But their husbands weren't interested in taking care of the families they had created. So what were these women going to do? And what would happen to the children? —Because of this treachery, **God rejected the offerings made by these men.**

> ***Because the Lord was*** *witness*
> *(to the covenant made at your marriage)*
> *between you and the wife of your youth,*
> *against whom you* ***have dealt treacherously***
> *and to whom* ***you were faithless.***
> *Yet she is your companion and the wife of your covenant*
> *(made by your marriage vows).*
>
>

Mal. 2:13-14 AMP

Offerings aren't bribes used to pay God to look the other way when we sin.

*But with Cain and **with his offering he was not pleased.***
So Cain was exceedingly displeased, and his countenance was sad.
And the Lord said to Cain, Why are you displeased? And
*why is your countenance sad? Behold, **if you do well, shall you not***
***be accepted?** And if you do not well, sin lies at the door.*
Gen. 4:5-7 LMSA

All farmers know that God provides the rain and sunshine, and without His help, the bugs would eat up their entire crop. Out of gratitude, the farmer (and all workers) offer Him a portion of what He has blessed them with. And it's not just any portion, it's what God puts into their hearts to give.

God is interested in obedience; not sacrifice. We give what He directs us to give. And we receive our needs met by asking Him what to do—and then by actually doing what He said.

Give, and it will be given unto you...
Luke 6:38

Since adultery threatens the future generation of the church, what does an (adulterous) person expect to receive by giving an offering? Especially if their ex-spouse is before God, crying on the altar:

if you are offering your gift at the altar
(and) there you ...remember that your brother (or spouse)
has something against you,
Leave your gift at the altar, and go.
***(and) make peace with your brother** (or spouse)*
and then come back and offer your gift.
Mat. 5:23-24

God Prevents Poverty—But, We Have to Do Our Part

*And **I will rebuke** the devourer (insects and plagues)*
for your sakes and he shall not destroy
the fruits of your ground,

> *neither shall your vine drop its fruit*
> *before the time in the field says the Lord of hosts*
>
> *Mal. 3:11*

According to Mal. 2:13-14, the adulterous spouse may have given God an offering (in church), but the devil and his demons will not be rebuked or **commanded by God not to steal, kill, or destroy** the unfaithful spouse's business, ministry, personal life, or health.

If the adulterous person wants the blessings of God to return, he (or she) must **repent**. However, if pride prevents them from repenting, then they've unconsciously chosen to live under the curse of Duet. 28.

We're created in the image and likeness of God. So if God is free to make decisions, so are we. **God doesn't use torture** to force us to do His Will. Instead, He respects our decisions, whether good or bad.

Whippings wont cause a slave to trust you. But if you set the slave free, and offer to help him succeed, then trust will develop, and so will admiration and love.

In helping us to make the right decision, He strongly commands **us to choose** life—to avoid the curse.

> *I call heaven and earth to bear witness against you this day,*
> *that I have set before you life and death, blessings and cursings;*
> ***therefore choose life, that both*** *you and your descendants* ***may live;***
>
> *Deut. 30:19 LMSA*

Practice Obeying the Voice
of the Holy Spirit

The Holy Spirit tells us what God wants us to know. So when we hear the voice of the Holy Spirit, we're really listening to God's thoughts and His instructions.

God can't force us to follow His instructions. But those who ask Him for something, and does what He says, **gets good results.**

Those who hear, but can't accept what God says as the truth, will experience the curse of Duet. 28 which is poverty, disease, and premature death. And the sad thing is, that some Christians will gladly obey the Lord, but there hasn't been much teaching on following the leading of the Holy Spirit.

> *Why do you call **Me**, Lord, Lord,*
> *and do not (**practice**) what **I** tell you?*
>
> > *Luke 6:46 AMP*

Notice that the Lord is saying to **practice** doing what **He** tells you...

> *For everyone who **comes to Me and listens** to My words...*
> *is like... a man building a house... and when a flood arose,*
> *the torrent broke against that house and could not shake or move it*

When we **practice** asking the Lord what to do, and doing what He tells us, we'll get good results. And each time this happens, it'll become easier to **identify His voice.** This is how we **gain confidence** in God and learn to trust Him.

> *But he who merely hears*
> *and **does not practice** doing My words*
> *is like a man who built a house...*
> *against which the torrent burst,*
> *and immediately it collapsed and fell,*
> *and the breaking and ruin of that house was great.*
>
> > *Luke 6:49 AMP*

People Who don't Know God Wont Trust Him

Normally, **we don't trust people we don't know—not even God.** This explains why some Christians are afraid to do what He says. But in order to know Him, we have to **practice doing what He says**, so we can see Him move. When He does, our confidence in Him will grow, and so will our trust. Look at it this way, what's the worse that can happen? If you're wrong, you'll only stay where you are. But if you're right, your life will change.

You can choose *"life and blessing"* 24-hours a day by seeking the wise counsel of God. And if you do what He says, your problems will be solved.

Putting God to the Test

"P*utting God to the test*" is willfully sinning. **It's knowing the will of God, but not doing it**, and waiting to see how far we can go without experiencing consequences.

When Jesus was tempted in the wilderness by satan, He said, **"I will not test the Lord my God."**

Mature Christians have decided to believe that God's Word is the truth. They believe that they're who the *Word* says they are, and they can do what the Word says they can do. By speaking God's exact words, and by following His instructions, they have discovered that **God will confirm (and prove) that His word is the truth by His actions.**

Baby Christians Play Games

Baby Christians (and sinners) know that God exist. But they play games to see how much they can get away with. This is because they haven't learned to trust Him, yet.

Look at Psalm 78:18-29 NIV

> *They willfully **put God to the test** by demanding the food they craved. They spoke against God, saying, "Can God spread a table in the desert?"*

A Slave (and Poverty) Mentality

When Moses parted the Red Sea, the Hebrews saw the power of God, and became aware of His capabilities. But satan fought tirelessly for their minds. He constantly reminded them of their poverty, their pain, and the deaths of their family members.

They had forgotten that during a famine, God told Isaac not to go into Egypt, but to **rely upon Him**. But Jacob broke his agreement (or covenant) with God when he moved into Egypt, **and his lack of trust in God led his descendants into slavery.**

Although they were freed, they couldn't rise above the slave or (poverty) mentality because satan kept saying: "How can you trust a God who could have prevented slavery in the first place?!"

They should have answered satan by saying:

> *"God told Abraham that his future descendants would go into slavery. But, He also said that He would set us free.*
>
> *Yes, Jacob moved into Egypt without asking God first, and that caused us to go into slavery. But God kept His promise to Abraham, and we are now free! And we're never going to be slaves again! Because this time, we're going to rely upon God!"*

Instead, they constantly questioned Moses about God's abilities. Then Moses became angry with them, and in his frustration, he disobeyed God by hitting the rock, instead of speaking to it:

> *When he (Moses) struck the rock*
> *water gushed out, and streams flowed abundantly.*

But water wasn't enough, they wanted more:

> **But can he also give us food? Can he supply meat for his people?"** *When the Lord heard them, he was very angry;*

> *...for **they did not believe in God or trust in his deliverance**.*
>
> *(vs. 20-22)*

Although He was angry, God decided to pass their test:

> *Yet **he gave a command** to the skies above*
> *...he rained, down manna for the people to eat,*
> *...he sent them all the food they could eat.*
>
> *(vs. 23-25)*

> *...He rained meat down on them like dust,*
>
> *(vs. 27)*
>
> *...They ate till they had more than enough*
> ***for he had given them what they craved***
>
> *(vs. 29)*

They refused to believe in His goodness, no matter what He did for them:

> *God's anger rose against them;*
> *He put to death the sturdiest among them,*
> *cutting down **the young men...**   .*
>
> *(vs. 31)*

> *In spite of all this, **they kept on sinning***
> *in spite of his wonders, **they did not believe***
>
> *(vs. 32)*

So they lived out their **average lives** in a wilderness, and died from old age; never having accomplished anything great.

> *Therefore **their days did he consume** in vanity (uselessness),*
> *and their years in trouble.*
>
> *Psalms 78:33 NIV*

Remaining Divorced for the Rest of Your Life

You may have divorced your spouse, or your spouse may have divorced you. And perhaps your ex-wife or (ex-husband) might have already gotten remarried. –So what are you going to do, remain single for the rest of your life?

If you choose to remain single for the rest of your life, that's fine, as long as it's the Will of God. But if you've decided to remain single, because you were taught that you're going to hell if you get remarried, then this book will show you what the Bible really says about getting remarried.

People are suppose to remain single for the rest of their lives, if God instructs them to (through *His word*, or through *a revelation*). But they're not suppose to allowed other people (including prophets) to choose this way of life for them.

If you've prayed about getting remarried, but haven't received an answer, it could be that you've already decided in your heart that if you got remarried, you're going to hell.

Jesus said, "...I am **the truth**..." Right? So let's look at the truth:

> *You have heard that it was said,*
> *You shall not commit adultery.*
>
> *Mat. 5:27 AMP*

> *But if the unbelieving partner leaves,*
> *(with no intentions of returning), let him do so;*
> *in such cases, the remaining (or innocent) brother or sister*
> *is not morally (or legally) bound*
> *(or tied together by a covenant),*
> *because God has called us to peace.*
>
> *1 Cor. 7:15*

ANSWERS TO HARD QUESTIONS

Q. **The Bible says that God has called us to peace. But how can I have peace when my spouse left, and made it clear that he's not coming back.**

Also, I'm afraid that if I get remarried, I'll be committing adultery, and go to hell.

A. God has called us to peace, but there is no peace when a husband or wife leaves. And how can there be peace if Christians want to get remarried, but believe that they'll go to hell?

For example:

> **John fell in love with Nydeera. So he divorced his wife, Martha, and married Nydeera**
>
> **ERRONEOUS traditional teaching MADE US THINK** that God would say to Martha:

"Because John has divorced you (so he could marry another woman) I will also punish you by not allowing you to get remarried. You will burn with sexual desire and passion, but you'll remain alone and childless for the rest of your life. And if you already have children, they'll remain fatherless! AND don't let the sun go down on your anger. Oh yeah!.. and don't even think about coveting your neighbor's husband."

Q. **Would God respond this way?**

A. Absolutely not! Because who would serve a God who wouldn't let them scratch when they itched, or not let them eat when they're hungry. Or refuse to forgive them when they truly repented. This is a monster, not the God that we serve.

Besides, it was John who refused to honor the Word of God; so he needs to repent. He violated God's word by looking to himself for love and sexual gratification, rather than looking to God to supply all of his needs.

Like any other sin, adultery can be forgiven, because in John 4:18 the woman at the well had been married five times. And the man she was living with, was not her husband.

There are Christians who disobey God by getting divorced and remarried regardless of His instructions. **But thank God Jesus died on the cross to provide forgiveness for all sins (including adultery).** And anyone who truly repents wont have to go to hell.

God also made **a way of escape** for the innocent spouse... It's called "remarriage."

> *...God is faithful, who will not suffer (or allow) you*
> *to be tempted above that ye are able; but will*
> *...make a way to escape, that ye may be able to bear it.*
>   *1 Cor. 10:13*

The purpose of getting remarried, is so that the innocent spouse can live the rest of his (or her) life in peace. You see, it's "the Covenant" that provides for us to have PEACE.

Therefore, Martha can **(peacefully) remain single, or she can get remarried** because she kept God's word and did nothing wrong to deserve being divorced. Also, her God-given covenant promises that she can live her life in **PEACE.** (See Mat. 5:27 and 1 Cor. 7:15 AMP)

After adultery is committed, it's hard to think that God wouldn't do anything about the innocent spouse's pain.

Q. Is John an unbeliever?

A.   Yes. Because he refuses to be led by the Holy Spirit. He also broke his promise to God, which is to love his wife like Christ loves the church. You see, a believer would obey God's word before hurting others.

Q.   Could John and Martha reconcile and remarry?

A.   Martha could pray for John to divorce his new wife and to marry her again—which is highly unlikely, but possible.

If this is the case, then Martha must be willing to wait for John, even if his marriage to Nydeera lasts for five, ten, or fifteen years.

In fifteen years, a lot of things could change. First of all, Martha's children will grow up and leave home for college. She will get older, and her views regarding life will change. For instance, she might lose interest in John after years of loneliness, and decide to remarry someone else.

Q.   What grounds do I have for getting divorced if my spouse makes me feel old and ugly, and he doesn't seem interested in me anymore?

When he's at home, he barely speaks, and he avoids being in the same room with me. I'm fed up, and I want a divorce!

A.   First, ask the Father if you should ask your spouse for a divorce. If the Holy Spirit gives you peace with your request, then ask for the proper time to talk to your spouse.

Asking for a divorce, most likely, will prompt your mate to ask, "Why?" This will lead to a discussion where you'd probably discover that your spouse might be experiencing difficulties in which he is embarrassed, or feels inadequate to talk to you about.

If both of you are believers, then you should be able to sit down and talk. Start by telling him how much you need him to talk to you, and assure him that you won't be critical or judgmental. Then after you talk, ask God what to do.

Q. What if my Christian husband takes his clothes and leaves? Should I remain unmarried, or should I pray for him to return?

A. If your husband is a Christian, God has already given him written instructions to follow:

> *Now to the married, I command (yet not I) but the Lord:*
> *...a husband is not to divorce (abandon, depart, or leave) his wife.*
> *1 Cor. 7:11*

If he's filled with the Holy Spirit, he'll be able to hear God's voice giving him instructions.

If your husband did something wrong, it's important that you forgive him because you'll need to hear God's voice, (so He can tell you what to do).

Each situation is different; for instance, you might be the one who did something wrong. If this is the case, you need to repent, and then ask God what to do to reconcile with your husband.

Q. How much authority does the church have over me and my spouse?

A. The Holy Spirit's job is to guide you to the church you're suppose to attend. Then the Pastor is responsible for teaching you about the Bible. After that, it's your job to **go home and study** those scriptures to prove that your Pastor has taught you the truth.

> *...they ...SEARCHED the scriptures daily*
> *TO FIND OUT whether these things were so.*
>
> *Therefore many of them believed.*
> *Acts 17:11-12 NKJV*

Your responsibility

It's your job to study the scriptures, pray, and obey God's instructions.

> *Do your best to present yourself to God as one approved,*
> *a workman who does not need to be ashamed*
> *and who correctly handles the word of truth*
>
> *2 Tim. 2:15 NIV*

The best way to study the Bible is to **divide it into parts**. For instance, if you want to know about divorce and remarriage, get a concordance and look up all the scriptures about "divorce" and "remarriage." Using this method, the Bible can be divided into many parts: the *healing* part, the *financial* part, the *family part, etc...*

Searching the scriptures is the only way to know if your pastor is teaching you the truth.

Some Christians are still being taught old wives tales, fables, and misquoted scriptures which are not found in the Bible. And this is why they haven't been getting good results. But if they would search the scriptures, then they would know the truth, which would set them free from wrong thinking.

> *...in the latter times, some will turn from the faith,*
> *giving heed to ...doctrines of demons (and one of them is)*
> ***forbidding people to marry...***
>
> *1 Tim. 4:1-3*

God's responsibility

God promised to supply all of your needs in Phil. 4:19 and in Isa. 58:11. Therefore, if you obey Him and follow His instructions, He promised to give you:

1. Peace, (Knowing you can remarry
   and have a happy family).   1 Cor. 7:15
2. Money   Isa. 45:3, Luke 6:38
3. Sexual fulfillment in marriage
   (In the Lord only)   1 Cor. 7:2
4. Companionship   Isa. 54:5 KJV
5. Step-parents for your children   Isa. 54:4
6. Security   Isa. 54:17, Isa. 46:4
7. Protection   Psalms 91

The Church's Responsibility

The church's job is to pray for you, and **to teach you how to live God's way**, so you can get good results in your life.

*And they went forth, and preached everywhere, the Lord working with them, and **(proving that His Word is the truth)** with SIGNS following.*

Mark 16:20

*Let the elders who rule well be counted worthy of double honor, especially those who labor in the word (**searching** the scriptures) and (**studying** the) doctrine.*

1 Tim. 5:17

Q. My Christian spouse divorced me, and remarried someone else. Does that make my ex-spouse an unbeliever?

A. If your ex-spouse was a believer, then he (or she) would have followed the instructions written in God's Word. Right?

*This is the covenant that I will make with them
 after those days, saith the Lord,
 I will put my laws into their hearts
 and **in their minds** will I write them;*

Hebrews 10:16

If your ex-spouse refused to honor the Word of God, or the leading of the Holy Spirit, then he (or she) is still living in disobedience, which is sin. He (or she) needs to repent and then follow the instructions of the Holy Spirit. And if you had anything to do with causing the divorce, then you need to repent also.

Taking Advantage of God's Mercy

Some people take advantage of God's mercy. **They sin on purpose, then they repent**. By doing this, they hope to get away with it. But God knows who's doing this, and **He will not allow His Saints to be the life-long victim of someone else's sin.**

> *For sin shall not [any longer] exert dominion over you...*
> *Rom. 6:14 AMP*

If your Christian spouse divorced you against the Will of God, and have already remarried someone else, then he (or she) needs to repent.

Later, he (or she) will need to ask for your forgiveness for the agony you've been put through. This is good, and it will help you to heal. But for your own sanity and peace of mind, God wants you to forgive him (or her).

Forgive, Forget, and Move on...

Rejection, betrayal, and adultery is always painful especially when you love the other person so much. But after several years, the pain leaves and you're ready for a new relationship. Only this time you're wiser, and wont let the same mistakes happen again.

It doesn't matter who messed up, or whether your ex-spouse is remarried or not; ...if he (or she) doesn't want to come back to you, or refuse to follow God's instructions, then...

You need to repent of your sins, forgive him (or her) for their sins, and then continue serving God.

Later, if you need a new spouse, ask God for one. And just like He gave you the first one, He'll give you another one.

And the wisdom here, is that next time, you'll work harder to make sure that your remarriage is a success. Right?

Shutting God Out is Dangerous

If Christians get divorced without God's approval, but later repents, they will be forgiven. But after they're forgiven, if they decide to shut God out (because they're afraid that He'll say to return home) then they'll be living in disobedience.

> *Don't trust your own understanding,*
> *...but, in everything you do, acknowledge me,*
> *and I will direct your path*

Prov. 3:5

Imagine the peace that comes with being in a friendly relationship with God. Your prayers are answered, your offerings are accepted, you're protected from your enemies, and you have His help, especially in times of trouble (like sickness or death).

Q.   Why do some churches teach that getting divorced is wrong?

A.   Some churches teach this because in Matthew 19:8-12 NIV, Jesus said:

> *...Moses permitted you to divorce your wives because your*
> *hearts were hard."*

(Vs. 8)

Moses got permission from God to allow the people to divorce and remarry because some couples found it difficult to live together. Others were going to sneak around and commit adultery anyway. So to prevent sin from being in the camp, God permitted them to get divorced. (Duet. 24:1).

The Bible doesn't encourage us to get divorced, instead, Jesus taught us to pray, and ask God what to do.

Some churches teach that getting divorced is wrong because after the divorce, the (once-again single) mother usually has to raise the children alone. So she'll turn to the church for financial assistance, counseling, child care, and emotional support. And sometimes she's ashamed because her husband begins dating someone in the same church. This is why the Bible says...

> **But it was not this way from the beginning.**
>
> *(Vs. 8)*

> Adam stayed with Eve, even though they were put out of the garden. And Noah took his beloved wife with him into the ark. And job didn't divorce his wife when she told him to curse God and die. And Abraham didn't divorce Sarah after he had a child with his other (Egyptian) wife; instead, they stayed together, and God fixed it.
>
> Isaac didn't divorce Rebecca, because he loved the wife that God had chosen for him. And although Jacob didn't love Leah, he didn't divorce her.
>
> Joseph didn't divorce his Egyptian (African) wife, when his (Hebrew) family came to Egypt. And Moses didn't divorce his (African) wife, although his (Hebrew) sister didn't like her.

Also in the New Testament, **there's no record of the Apostles getting divorced,** because Jesus taught them this:

> *"I tell you that anyone who divorces his wife,*
> *...(except for marital unfaithfulness)*
> *and marries another woman commits adultery."*
>
> *(Vs. 9)*

His disciples didn't like this commandment; look at what they said:

The disciples said to him, "If this is the situation between a husband and wife, it is better not to marry."

(Vs. 10)

The disciples (who had normal sex drives) decided that remaining single was better than getting married and being stuck with one wife for the rest of their lives. But Jesus replied:

"Not everyone can accept this word (the idea of remaining single for a life time), **but only those to whom (the gift of celibacy) has been given."** **(Vs. 11)**

Q. **Do people get divorced because their spouse doesn't give them enough SEX?**

A. **Yes!** Some people expect their spouses to understand that they're tired from working all day, and don't feel like having sex. Or, they have to work out-of-town for two or three weeks, so there will be no sex. But always assuming that your strong Christian spouse will wait until tomorrow, or next week, or next month, is dangerous!

Now, let's see what God says about this:

*Do not deprive one another except when both of you **consent** to do so, especially at the time when you devote yourselves to **fasting and prayer**; and then come together again, so that satan may not **tempt you** because of your **physical passion**.*

1 Cor. 7:5 LMSA

God said that you must be in agreement not to have sex (so you can fast and pray). He didn't say because you're tired. And He didn't say because you have to work out-of-town for two months.

Beloved, satan doesn't care if you were busy with the kids all day, or out making a lot of money. You're being watched, and he knows what's going on, and he'll send someone to tempt you or your spouse. So make time for sex!

There are spiritual guidelines for **SEX** that we must follow in order to please God. Yes! The Kingdom of God has laws, that once followed, yields a harvest of pleasure, peace, comfort, contentment, happiness and joy. Money and pornography can make you feel good, but it can't release stress and give you the pleasure and peace that comes from having sex.

> *Nevertheless, to avoid fornication, let every man have his own wife, and let every woman have her own husband.*
>
> *Let the husband render unto the wife due benevolence: and likewise also the wife unto the husband.*
>
> *1 Cor. 7:2, 3*

Don't give satan an opportunity to make either of you want a divorce.

If there is already a problem, I advise you to seek Professional Christian Counseling. Divorce is not the only answer. Why? Because you and your mate must get to the root or source of the problem. Once you identify the root of the problem, then get into a Prayer of Agreement. Open your mouths **and use the power of God's Word to change your circumstances.**

> Open your mouths and confess your love for your spouse.
>
> Women, confess that your husband loves you like Christ loves the church.
>
> And men, confess that your wives love you and will always respect you.
>
> So when satan comes along speaking ugly words of negativity, ignore him completely and start talking to God about what you believe.

PUT ME IN REMEMBRANCE OF MY WORD.

Isa. 62:6

Open your Bible, and find the place where God promised to bless your sex life. For example...

> *"Let your fountain (sexual organ) be blessed,*
> *and rejoice with the wife of your youth."*
>
> *Prov. 5:18*

This promise is included in your covenant, so ask for it! And expect God to use His awesome powers to get it for you.

Q.   Is Denominational Differences A Reason For Divorce

A.   For centuries, men have been using the Bible to support their own ideas. And some of these rules that they make up are very difficult for people to keep.

Some Christians never get remarried. They spend twenty or thirty years alone, without having children. But one morning they'll wake up and realize that in order to be a good Christian, all they had to do was repent, and then follow God's instructions on how to have a happy and fulfilling life.

> *Without faith, it is impossible to please God.*
>
> *Heb. 11:6*

Beloved, in the Name of Jesus Christ, OPEN Your Bible and READ IT for yourself! Then pray in the spirit for understanding and wisdom.

> ***Study** to shew yourself approved unto God, a workman that needeth not to be ashamed, but rightly dividing the Word of Truth.*
>
> *II Tim. 2:15*

When studying the Bible, it should be divided into sections. For instance:

> Marriage, divorce, sex, children, fertility, healing,
> money, business, miracles, joy, obedience, faith,
> and the gifts of the spirit, etc...

Of course, there are hundreds of sections–but I'm making a point, which is to STUDY the Bible for yourself!   And become like thousands of Christians who have accepted God's forgiveness for **their past** sins, and have moved on with their lives.

Always compare scriptures so that you get the whole picture.

Q.   Does my spouse have the God-given right to punish me (by leaving) and causing me to live alone for the rest of my life?

And what am I suppose to do if I have sexual tension and emotional pain as a result of being left alone?

A.   *For the wife does not have (exclusive) authority and control over her own body, but **the husband (has his rights)**;*

*likewise also the husband does not have (exclusive) authority and control over his body, but **the wife (has her rights)**.*

Sex is not a weapon to be used to punish the husband, or to hurt the wife. Love, attention, and affection are gifts from God, and should be used in marriage to provide intimacy and pleasure.

> *Do not refuse and deprive and defraud each other [of your due marital rights]*
>
> *1 Cor. 7:4-5 AMP*

The husband has power over the wife's body, and she has power over his. But when one spouse doesn't make him (or herself) available for affection, it causes the other spouse physical and emotional pain.   —**And no one is authorized by God to afflict pain on anyone else.**

Marriage is not a game.   When two consenting adults agree to share everything together, but one of them violates this agreement, then someone (including the children) gets hurt.

That's why prayer is very important, because it gives the Holy Spirit an opportunity to warn us if we're headed towards problems.

If you married someone (against the advise of the Holy Spirit) and the marriage ends in divorce, God will forgive you because you didn't commit the unpardonable sin. But this type of disobedience can produce consequences that you might have to live with for a long time (like being a single parent until God blesses you with another spouse).

Without remarriage, many Christians would suffer a lifetime of loneliness; and in some cases, childlessness.

Q. If a Christian makes a mistake, or a bad decision, does this mean that he (or she) is a sinner or an unbeliever?

A.   No. Because when we repent, God forgives us.

> *If we confess our sins,*
> *He is faithful and just to forgive our sins*
> *and to cleanse us from all unrighteousness.*
>
> *1 John 1:9*

> *I write to you, little children, because*
> ***your sins are forgiven you for His name's sake.***
>
> *1 John 2:12*

When Christians repent, they are forgiven, and their friendship with God is restored.

You see, true repentance is when we make a decision (in our hearts) to stop sinning. But a believer is considered **a backslider** when he or she repents (but have no real intention of doing what's right).

A backslider refuses to obey the Holy Spirit, and causes people unnecessary pain. This is a believer who ignores the teachings of Jesus, and therefore, is acting worst then an infidel **(or an unbeliever)**. 1 Tim. 5:8.

Q. **When will God permit a divorce?**

A. Eventually, God will permit a divorce when one spouse leaves with no intention of returning. Or, continues to commit adultery, or is constantly violent, or grossly neglects his (or her) spouse.

You should seek the wisdom of God (in prayer) before deciding to reconcile, because God knows if your spouse is really ready to commit.

If you are the spouse of an adulterous mate, you'll be able to remarry according to 1 Cor. 7:15, because God wants you to have peace and happiness in this life. **And when God blesses you with another mate, you will not be living in adultery**.

> *...the believing brother or sister is not in bondage (to stay married to an adulterous spouse, because) God has called us to (live in) peace.*
>
> *1 Cor. 7:15*

Q. **I'm a Christian who caused my divorce by committing adultery. But my spouse doesn't want to take me back. What should I do?**

A. **If you're a Christian who's responsible for the divorce because you committed adultery,** then ask God for forgiveness. —Then receive His forgiveness, and believe that He has restored you to a position of "righteousness." Later, you'll need to ask your ex-husband (or ex-wife) for forgiveness.

If your spouse doesn't want to take you back, then talk to God about it. Only He can lead and guide you (through the Holy Spirit). And only He can make your spouse return, but if he (or she) rejects the leading of the Holy Spirit, then God will show you what He wants you to do.

If your Christian ex-husband (or ex-wife) divorced you without talking to God about it first; and if he (or she) has already remarried someone else, then your (ex) needs to repent.

Unless God separates two Christians, getting married to anyone else will be living in adultery.

Q.   Can I divorce my spouse if he (or she) is sentenced to **several years**, or **life imprisonment**, or gets the **death penalty**?

What am I suppose to do when **I want to have sex** at night?

A.   God knows that your spouse is in prison, and how long he
(or she) will be there. He also knows how long you can wait.
And since He's the only one qualified to tell you all the details
concerning your life, be honest with Him in prayer, and expect
Him to answer you...

In all your ways acknowledge Him,
and He will direct your path.

Prov. 3:6

 No one can answer these questions for you because God has already said:

...seek ye first the kingdom of God, and his righteousness;
and all these things (everything) will be added (or given) unto you.
Mat. 6:33

God said to come to Him (first), and He will give you the answer. He didn't say to call a friend, because **He never promised to work in your life according to your friend's advise.**

After seeking Him, He might lead you to someone whose advice will be in agreement with what the Bible says.

REMARRIAGE

Remarriage is Practiced in the New Testament

Jesus said to her, Go and call your husband, and come here.
*She said to him, I have **no husband**.*
Jesus said to her, You said well, I have no husband;
*For **you have had five husbands;***

Legally, this woman was **divorced and remarried five times;** and Jesus never denied it.

and the one you now have is not your husband;
what you said is true.

John 4:16-18 LMSA

Under the Old Testament Law, if this woman hadn't been **legally divorced**, she and her lover would have been stoned for **committing adultery**.

After her statement, *"I have no husband,"* Jesus points out that she was presently living with an unmarried man **in fornication**. (He only did this to prove to her that He was the Messiah). Then she said:

...I know that the Messiah (Christ) is coming;
*when he is come, **he will teach us everything**.*
*Jesus said to her, **I am he** who is speaking to you.*

John 4:25-26 LMSA

In the New Testament **any adulterous person who truly repents will receive mercy and forgiveness.** Afterwards, **if the forgiven person**

desires to be remarried, God might lead him (or her) back to their ex-spouse (depending upon the circumstances); or He'll bless them with a different Christian mate. How can this be? Well, let's look at the Benefits Jesus provided:

> *Bless the Lord, O my soul, and forget not **all his benefits**,*
> ***Who forgives all** your iniquities,*
> *who **heals all** your diseases.*
> ***Who redeems (or rescues) your life** from destruction,*
>
> *Psalm 103:2-4*

God said that one of His benefits was FORGIVENESS. And look, another benefit is HEALING!

> *And the prayer of faith will **heal** the sick,*
> *and our Lord will raise him up;*
> *and **if he has committed sins**,*
> *he will be forgiven.*
>
> *James 5:15 NKJV*

And still another benefit is RECOVERING from destruction. This means that all Christians can be forgiven and receive a second chance **(including those who have messed up their marriage(s)**.

It's no different than people who eat junk food for most of their lives and later develop some kind of illness. These people are still entitled to recover from destruction although they caused the problem. And that's not all, God will also show them how to eat right.

Remarriage was Practiced in the Old Testament

> *If **a man takes a wife**, and lies with her,*
> *and if she finds no favor in his eyes,*
> *because he has found some evidence of open prostitution in her;*
> *then let him **write her a bill of divorcement**,*
> *and give it to her, and send her out of his house.*

> *...if she goes and becomes another man's wife,*
> *And if that husband hates her, and*
> **writes her a bill of divorcement**, *and gives it to her...*

In the Old Testament, divorced women and widows were allowed to remarry. But widows weren't allowed to remarry their ex-husbands.

> *...or if **that husband** who took her to be his wife **dies;***
> *Then **her former husband**, who sent her away*
> *has no right to take her again to be his wife.*
>
> *Duet. 24:3-4 LMSA*

When Not to Get Married

It's good that people are turning back to marriage; however, there are some marriages that shouldn't take place:

Like the people who get married even though they heard the Holy Spirit say, "**No!**" in prayer.

And those who have **no peace** with the idea of marrying a certain person.

Some Christians got married because they had sex, or children out-of-wedlock. Knowing that the Bible says, *...marriage is honorable, and the bed undefiled,* they tried to make things right by getting married, hoping this would please God...

But the only way to ensure that the marriage will work, and that the children wont be destroyed (by growing up in a hostile environment) is to ask God if the other person is right for you.

Having sex, or getting pregnant doesn't guarantee that people will stay together.

In wrong-relationships, people get beat up emotionally, and sometimes physically. They're encouraged to close their Bibles, and stop going to church. Then they're invited to destroy themselves by drinking alcohol, smoking weed, snorting cocaine, shooting heroine, or taking Meth (just to make the other person happy). But if they refuse, then there will be...

Arguing, fighting, cursing, adultery, cutting up each other's clothes, and destroying property, etc. What kind of relationship is this!?

Centering your life around God is the only way to prevent this type of activity in your marriage. But if satan is left to wreak havoc, he'll even suggest that a third-party be brought to bed, or something sexual that will violate your conscience.

If a Christian goes along with these no-good demands, **satan will back his truck up to that household and steal, kill, and destroy everything he gets his hands on.** (John 10:10)

Choosing the Right Person to Marry

How do you know if you're marrying the right person? First of all, God will lead you to the right person. And although you might not agree with His choice, things will just fall in place. Many happily married Christians started out not liking each other, but eventually (with little effort of their own) they became friends. And soon, the friendship turned into a romance which led to marriage.

Some Christians fight against marrying the person God has chosen. But through dreams, visions, or the Word, or in many other ways, God will get the point across that this is the right person for them to marry. And when they cooperate, a sweet union will be formed.

Q.   My church teaches against divorce and remarriage, but I remarried anyway, and it didn't work out. Is this because I disobeyed the church's teaching?

A.   There are several reasons why your (re)marriage could have ended in divorce.

If you trusted God to select your mate, yet the marriage ended in divorce, it was probably because you were in an environment that condemns remarriage.

> If you're in a church that teaches against remarriage, it's wise to pray and ask God for a new church where your (re)marriage is accepted and celebrated. Also, it might be necessary to limit your visits to friends and relatives who have strong feelings against your decision, because every new relationship needs a healthy environment in order to grow.

However, if you married an unbeliever, there were probably many things that came between the two of you...

> Such as a difference in beliefs, and a lack of interesting things to do. For instance, on weekends one goes to church alone, and the other person goes to parties alone. This lack of interest in each other's fun-filled activities, probably left very little to discuss during dinner.

Perhaps you thought that you could change him (or her) after you were married, but later discovered that you couldn't.

If your spouse had sex with you while he (or she) was married to someone else, then he (or she) will probably commit adultery after marrying you.

Although your marriage ended in divorce, don't loose confidence in God. He's still good, and will lead you to greener pastures.

Q. **I was deeply hurt after my divorce, and now I'm afraid that if I remarry it might happen again. I have been alone for so many years, and now I'm old and unattractive.**

A. If God puts remarriage in your spirit, then you should cooperate with Him. He already knows how long you can remain alone. If you refuse, **where does this put you for the rest of your life?**

What if God hasn't given you the gift of celibacy? What if you prefer to live married, and enjoy having sex? This doesn't describe a person who wants to live alone for the rest of his (or her) life.

God healed you from sickness so you could serve Him without pain. And He delivered you from poverty, so you could serve Him with generosity. And He's saving you from premature death (when you follow His instructions) so you can finish your assignment.

Jesus came to give you a life better than the one you're living now. **A life filled with purpose.** By His death on Calvary, He unlocked the handcuffs, shackles, and restraints that satan used to make you unproductive.
Look at the compassion of the Messiah.

> *As he approached the town gate, a dead person was being carried out—the only son of his mother, and she was a widow.*
>
> *...When the Lord saw her,* **his heart went out to her** *and he said,* **"Don't cry."**
>
> *Then he went up and touched the coffin, and those carrying it stood still. He said, "Young man, I say to you, get up!"*
>
> *The dead man sat up and began to talk,*
> *and **Jesus gave him back** to his mother.*
> *Luke 7:12-15 NIV*

Jesus raised the young man from the dead because God didn't want the woman in pain. He didn't want her to cry. He didn't want her to be alone. So He restored her son's life to make her happy again. Jesus said:

> *"...**My father** has worked [even] until now,*
> *[He has never ceased working; **He is still working**]*
> *and I, too, must be at divine work.*
> *John 5:17 AMP*

God lives in Jesus, and Jesus lives in you. This is where your ability to do the impossible comes from.

While praying to His Father, Jesus said:

> *I in them* and *You in Me*,
> *in order that they may become one*
> *and perfectly united...*
>
> *John 17:23 AMP*

This is why you can **experience a resurrection in your appearance and self-esteem**. And the reason you can trust God in every area of your life is because...

> *...He is God in Heaven above, and He is God on Earth beneath...*
> *Joshua 2:11*

In John 10:30, Jesus said:

> *"I and my Father are one."*

After Jesus ascended into Heaven, it became our responsibility to get sinners saved. But if they see us crying and begging, how will they believe that God will use His powers to heal them, or prosper them financially, and bless them with a long life. That's why it's extremely important for you to find out through prayer why God called you into a relationship with Him. And does He want you to remain single, or get remarried. –Don't delay!

Q. **If a divorced woman gets remarried, will she be living in adultery?**

A. – Not if the Holy Spirit allows her to divorce her husband because he's constantly committing adultery.
– And not if her husband divorced her to marry another woman.
– And not if her (Christian or unsaved) husband abandoned her (legally for one year).

Also, a divorced woman will not be living in adultery:

  – **if she repents** for committing adultery, or
  – **repents** for divorcing her husband and remarrying another man.

Remember, **adultery is not the unpardonable sin—which means it's a sin that can be forgiven.** Once she is forgiven of adultery, she must begin to obey the voice of the Holy Spirit. He might direct her to return to her first husband, or to remain alone, or to remain married to the second husband.

If the adulteress does not repent, then she will eventually die in her sins and go to hell. And it's the same for a man.

> *If we confess our sins, He is faithful and just to forgive us*
> *...and to cleanse us from all unrighteousness.*
>   *1 John 1:9*

Before we decide to divorce our mates to marry someone else, remember that the consequences of adultery are serious. Not only does it leave behind a broken-hearted spouse, but confused children who will later divorce their spouses for other men and women. This is not the plan of God for the Christian family. That's why the Bible says,

> *Give no offense ...**to the church of God**,*
> *just as I also please all men in all things,*
> *not seeking my own profit, but the profit*
> *of many, that they may be saved.*
>   *1 Cor. 10:33*

Let's look at Luke 16:18.

> *"Whoever divorces his wife and marries another (woman)*
> *commits adultery...*

This scripture means that a husband can not divorce his wife, so he can marry another woman. If he does, God considers him an adulterer. And if he marries the other woman, God doesn't see him as a legally-married man. Why? Because if God chose a wife for him, then He expects the man to use his faith, and trust His Father to fix the problem (and not break his covenant, agreement, or promise) which he made when he agreed to marry God's daughter.

> *...the Lord has been witness between you and the wife*
> *of your youth, with whom you have dealt treacherously;*
> *yet she is your companion and your wife by covenant.*
> *Malachi 2:14*

Now, let's go to the last part of Luke 16:18.

> **...and whoever marries her who is divorced from her husband commits adultery.**
> *Luke 16:18*

You see, this is talking about a woman who openly commits adultery, hoping that her husband will divorce her so she can marry her lover. And if she marries her lover, they will both be living in adultery.

Mat. 5:32 says the same thing:

> **...and whoever marries a woman who is divorced commits adultery.**
> *Mat. 5:32*

It's important to know that sexual immorality is a reason to get divorced, and that God will not punish the innocent spouse to remain alone and childless for the rest of his (or her) life.

Q. I was a sinner when I got divorced. But now I'm a Christian, and I want to get remarried. What does the Bible say about that.

A. If you caused your divorce when you were a sinner, but now you're a Christian who desires to get remarried, all you have to do is pray, and ask God what to do. If you desire to get remarried, Mark 11:24 says...

Whatsoever things you desire when you pray,
believe that you will get it,
and [then] it will be given to you."

There is nothing to hard for God—no matter what it is. And no sin is so griev-
ous that a man (or woman) has to remain childless and without comfort
for his (or her) **entire life**.

**Q.   I have never been married. Is it a sin to marry a divorced per-
son?**

A.   ...*ART THOU LOOSED (divorced) FROM A WIFE?*

Seek not an(other) wife.

BUT and *iF thou MARRY (RE-marry),*
THOU HAST NOT SINNED;

It is clear here that the scripture is referring to men who have been divorced from
their wives. It says that if a divorced man gets (re)married, he has not sinned!

and if a VIRGIN MARRY, she has not sinned.
Nevertheless such shall have trouble in the flesh;
BUT I SPARE YOU.

(1 Cor. 7:27-28)

God's remedy for "trouble-in-the-flesh," is marriage.

Now, let's see what this scripture does NOT say:

This scripture doesn't say that a virgin must marry another virgin.

Nor does it say that she must not marry a widower or a divorcee.

The Bible does say in 2 Cor. 6:14, not to marry unbelievers.

Be ye not unequally yoked together with unbelievers.

SEPARATION

When storms come, it's time to grab hold of the steering wheel and guide the ship through the storm. In the Kingdom of God, the steering wheel is your tongue. So only say what God said. And if the Holy Spirit reveals something to you, hang onto those words, and expect it to happen; because it will!

Just because brother and sister so-and-so's marriage ended in divorce, doesn't mean that yours will. Ask God to tell you why brother so-and-so's marriage ended. Once He tells you, then fear will no longer hold you in bondage.

Perhaps you counseled brother and sister so-and-so, but their marriage still ended in divorce. You might even see sister so-and-so everyday, and she doesn't look well. Her children might be neglected. Her home might be broken up. And you might feel that it's your fault, but until you ask God, the enemy will continue to plague you with guilt.

Four Reasons Why Christians Separate

Some Christians are tired of problems; like unfulfilling jobs, out-of-control teens, not enough money, illnesses, deaths, and crime in the community. They just want to get away from it all, and start over without the drama.

Angry Christians separate when they don't know what God has to say about their problems.

Some have experienced the pain of rejection and abandonment in the past, and fearing it will happen again, they run away.

Some become impatient waiting for their ministries to grow. They give up, and want to start their lives over again.

Pray Before You Separate

Before packing your clothes and leaving, get alone and pray. God says, "Lean not to your own understanding, in ALL of your ways, acknowledge me, and I will direct your path (throughout this life)."

When you pray in tongues, you are praying the perfect will of God. Once you receive revelation knowledge, wisdom, and understanding, you'll know what to do. If God tells you to separate, He'll tell you what to say, and where to go.

In 1 Cor. 7:11, God tells the husband, "Don't divorce your wife" without first seeking the Wise Counsel of God.

> *Seek ye FIRST...*
> *Mat. 6:33*

Q. **I've separated from my spouse because of adultery and verbal abuse. But I'm lonely now. Must I be punished because of someone else's disobedience to God.**

A. Thus saith the Lord:

It is my desire to give you the best of everything, saith the Lord. But you will not hear me, you will not heed my words. How many times have I spoken to you, yet you would not listen. However, you've listened to the voice of religion, paganism, and the sort. But you would not hear me.

God's best for you includes the rarest and most unusual husband who is proud to call you his wife.

Your obedience to God, your trust, your dependency, and your praises will cause His presence to fill your home with love, peace, compassion, and joy. His incomparable wisdom will teach you how to fill every room of your house with the finest quality. He'll provide you with work that you love and good health to enjoy it all. It's not difficult to follow the Holy Spirit whose job is to lead you to your God-given inheritance.

You are rewarded with the best of everything for carefully listening to HIS VOICE, and carrying out His will.

Dishonorable Relationships

1 Cor. 7:27 says Christians must not divorce in order to re-marry another person. In such case, the marriage would not be honorable in the sight of God, and the bed would be defiled. So creating a new relationship by dis-obeying God would not exactly overwhelm Him with joy.

> *And unto the married I command, yet not I, but the Lord,*
> *Let not the wife depart from her husband:*
>
> *But, and if, she depart, let her remain unmarried,*
> *or be reconciled to her husband:*
> *and let not the husband put away (divorce) his wife.*
>
> *1 Cor. 7:10-11*

If two believers divorced without the permission of God, although neither committed adultery, God's word says in (vs. 11) *"...remain unmarried or be reconciled"* and in (vs. 27) it says, *"...seek not a wife."* God specifically commands the husband not to divorce his wife. This is because God has a plan, but it's our responsibility to find out what it is.

Unavoidable Separations

> *To the married I give this command (not I, **but the Lord**): A wife must not separate from her husband. But if she does, she must remain unmarried or else be reconciled to her husband. And a hus-band must not divorce his wife.*
>
> 1 Cor. 7:10-11 NIV

Although the Bible advises us not to separate, there are times when it's impossible to remain together.

From the scripture above, we can conclude that God decides who splits up and who remains married. Notice that in (vs. 11) married people are instructed to:

1. **Remain unmarried**— because their God-given assignment with that spouse hasn't been completed yet. You see, God, as well as the children, are also involved in this marital relationship.

2. **Be reconciled** to her husband (or to his wife) to avoid adultery, disease, and unwanted children.

    "But you don't know what it's like to live with so-and-so!" you might be saying. You're right. I don't know. But for God to say **"remain unmarried"** or **"be reconciled,"** we can safely assume that He has the solution to fix the problem.

Forgiving Your Spouse for Committing Adultery, Child Abuse, or Rape

What if God wants you to forgive your spouse for committing adultery? Didn't Christ die so the Father could forgive your sins?

God has asked people to forgive their spouses for committing adultery, rape, and child abuse. In most of these cases, the families became involved in Christian counseling, and many needed rehabilitation from drugs or alcohol. And some forgave; but disobeyed God and got divorced, and moved away.

When couples forgive and reconcile, God provides them with an abundance of GRACE or FAVOR.

On the other hand, if one of them refuse to reconcile, this will eventually cause the (willing-and-obedient) spouse to fall into temptation and commit adultery.

What God has put together, he warned, "*Let no man put asunder.*" This means that the couple must work hard to stay together. If there is a problem, God wants them to seek Him for wisdom.

Dating a Married Man
Who's Separated From His Wife

Here's scriptural wisdom for the single person (who's dating a married Christian). Especially if the married Christian is promising to marry you, and threatening to divorce his wife (or her husband):

> *We know that whosoever is born of God sinneth not;*
> *but **he that is begotten of God keepeth himself,***
> *and that wicked one toucheth him not.*
>
> *1 John 5:18*

Did you know that satan is really trying to stop the work of God in your life. (Rom. 8:8)

Also, if this Christian divorces his wife to marry you, it's likely that he'll continue to commit adultery after marrying you.

It's time for the two of you to repent. And you need to ask God to bless you with your own husband (or wife).

Q. My husband was separated when we met. Then he divorced his wife and married me. Neither of us were aware of 1 Cor. 7:10-11. What are we suppose to do?

A.   If your relationship with him was the reason he separated from his wife, the Bible says to repent.

If your husband didn't try to pray or reconcile with his ex-wife before filing for a divorce, he has to repent too.

And if the ex-wife did anything to cause the divorce, she needs to repent.

But if the ex-wife is innocent, you and your new husband should ask her for forgiveness (but do it separately).

If there's any children from the first marriage, they'll need their father in their lives, and he has to make sure that child support is provided for them.

Although you and your husband have (re)married, it's good to know what the Bible says about separation and divorce.

Q.   We've been separated for nine months, and neither of us want to reconcile. We want to move on with our lives. So how do we know if we're suppose to get divorced.

A.   *But **if the unbelieving depart**,*
let him (or her) depart.
A BROTHER or A SISTER
<u>is not under bondage</u> in such cases:
but God has CALLED US TO PEACE.

1 Cor. 7:15

Not under bondage means that after one year, a **Christian husband (or wife)** has <u>legal</u> grounds to divorce an unbelieving spouse who separates, leaves, or abandons them with no intention of returning. They don't call, they don't write, they don't visit, they don't support the children. Perhaps they remarried someone else. In other words, they've made it clear that they never want to be in a relationship with you again.

A *bound* person is NOT FREE to enjoy his or her life. A *bound* person is tied up, held down, imprisoned, or enslaved.

In a separation, if any sexual activity is to take place, God said to RECON-CILE which means to *make up and get back together.* If the departed mate refuses to return and reconcile, this person is DISOBEYING THE WORD OF GOD.

> *And unto the married I command, yet not I, but the Lord,* **Let not the wife depart from her husband:**
>
> *But and* **if she depart, let her remain unmarried,** *or* **be reconciled to her husband***:*
>
> *1 Cor. 7:10-11*

Since God called his children to live in PEACE, the departed or disobedient spouse is guilty of another sin. He (or she) is robbing a child of God of his or her right to have PEACE. But before the divorce papers are filed, God must be consulted, because the Bible says...

> *and* **let not the husband put away (divorce) his wife***.*
>
> *1 Cor. 7:11*

Consulting God just means to talk to Him about the situation. Tell Him your desires to have a mate, to have sex, to have companionship, to have help, or to have a mother or father for your children; whatever the need is.

> *It shall come to pass That before they* **call, I will answer***; And while they are still speaking,* **I will hear***.*
>
> *Isa. 65:24*
>
> *He will* **fulfill the desire** *of those who fear Him; He also will hear their cry* **and save them***.*
>
> *Psalm 145:19*

The living God will answer you. If He says, "divorce," then ask Him, "Where do I go to file for a divorce?" He will send you to a place that is affordable and convenient. On the other hand, if Divorce Papers are served to you, the Lord will tell you what to do with them.

Separated for Years, Now what?

Perhaps you still love your spouse and don't want a divorce. But 1 year, 2 years, and maybe even 5 years later, if your mate hasn't returned, should you continue to put your life on hold?

Bondage is when you've been indoctrinated to believe that you are to remain SEPARATED and ALONE forever!

> Has your spouse found someone new?
> Is he (or she) sexually active?
> If so, adultery is grounds for a divorce.

If he (or she) is not sexually active, or you haven't the slightest idea, then ask yourself:

> Do I have peace with my spouse's decision to leave me alone for all of these years?"
>
> What is the Holy Spirit leading me to do?
> Do I understand the scriptures about getting divorced?
>
> Did I pray for wisdom so I'll know how to get my needs met?

ADULTERY

Adultery is not the unpardonable sin

Adultery occurs when a married person invites another person into his (or her) heart or bed. It also involves ignoring and rejecting ones spouse for the affection and attention of another. Adultery **is not the unpardonable sin,** and can be forgiven by both God and spouse.

Divorce is legally terminating the marriage *Agreement*. Legal grounds are adultery, separation, and irreconcilable differences.

Irreconcilable differences is when it's absolutely impossible for two people to get along. Sometimes neglect, violence, hatred, and abuse are involved. Especially when the abusive spouse refuses to ask God for help, or refuses to get professional counseling.

Here's a Biblical example of **irreconcilable differences**: 1 Cor. 7:15

> BUT if the **unbelieving** *(mate)*
> **departs** *(abandons, reject or **leaves you**)*,
> a brother or a SISTER *(Christian)*
> is not *(and hasn't been created or born-again to live...)*
> UNDER *(Or be subjected to, or submit to)*
> **bondage** *(a life-time of loneliness, depression, and mental anguish)*
> in such cases *(where the unbeliever no longer wants to be married)*
> BUT, *(instead)*
> God has called *(designated, appointed, selected, chosen)*
> us *(Christians)*
> to *(**live our Christian experience in**)*
> peace *(happiness, agreeing with God, and having our needs met)*.

Pornography and Internet Sex

You have heard that it is said, You shall not commit adultery.
*But I say to you that **whoever looks** at a woman **with lust**,*
*has already **committed adultery** with her **in his heart**.*

Mat. 5:27-28

Married people are guilty of adultery when they *intentionally* watch X-rated movies, or SEX websites, or read pornography. Some R-rated movies are also dangerous for Christians to watch because *...faith comes by hearing*. Movies involving **cursing, sex, and violence** invite our flesh to rebel against the commandments of God.

How A Man Causes His Wife to Commit Adultery

But I say to you that whoever divorces his wife,
***except for sexual immorality;** (having sex with another man)*
causes her to commit adultery;

Mat. 5:32

When a man divorces his wife for reasons other than adultery, he might be leaving behind a woman who's still in love with him. Also, she may still be dependent upon him sexually, emotionally, and financially.

In her heart, she's still married to him when she bows down to sexual temptation (with another man). Low self-esteem plagues her as she struggles to raise their children alone. This could have been prevented if the husband had trusted God.

According to 1 Cor. 7:15, **this woman can remarry; but she doesn't** because she's still in love with her ex-husband.

Adultery Can Be Forgiven

While teaching in the temple, **Jesus forgave a woman** who was caught in the very act:

> *Then the scribes and pharisees brought*
> *a woman who was caught in adultery;*
> *and they made her to stand in the midst. They said to him, Teacher,*
> ***this woman was caught openly in the act of adultery.***
> *Now **in the law of Moses** it is commanded*
> *that **women such as these** should be stoned;*
> ***but what do you say?***
>
>

John 8:3-5 LMSA

Jesus was going to die; and since adultery wasn't the only sin He was going to die for, He said:

> ***He who is** among you **without sin**,*
> *let him **first throw a stone at her.***
>
> *When Jesus straightened himself up, he said to the woman, Where are they? Did no man condemn you?*
> *She said, No man, Lord.*
>
> *Then Jesus said, **Neither do I condemn you;***
> *go away, and from henceforth, **do not sin again**.*
>
>

John 8:7, 10, 11 LMSA

Did Jesus say:

> "As long as you live, you may never become another man's wife. And if you don't have any children, shame on you! Because you'll never have a child in this life?"

No, Jesus never said that. Instead He said:

> **"Neither do I condemn (or curse) you."**

Adultery can be forgiven, but if it's continued, people will find themselves in situations from which they can't recover. Such as being disrespected by the people they love, acquiring an incurable disease, getting divorced, or not receiving answers to their prayers:

> *But whoso committeth adultery with a woman*
> *lacketh understanding:*
> *he that doeth it destroyeth his own soul.*
> *A wound and dishonor shall he get;*
> *and **his reproach shall not be wiped away**.*
>
> *Prov. 6:32, 33*

FAMILY PROBLEMS

Becoming A Step-parent

When it comes to raising someone else's kids, it's not easy. It's like walking onto a stage in the middle of a play. All you can do is perform your role and recite your part. You didn't write the play, you just got married, and became one of the actors in your step-child's life.

With your own children, you've been in control since they were born. But with your step-children, you had no control over the people who played important roles in their development. Nor did you have control over the environment in which they were raised. Had you been in control, you would have done things differently—but you weren't.

Get to Know Your Step-Children

Many people played a part in shaping the lives of your step-children. So in order to understand them better, try talking to some of the people who helped to raise them.

With a young step-child, try talking to the baby sitters, or the daycare center teacher. If the child is older, you can talk to the teachers, coaches, the former pastor, or youth leader. Ask if the child enjoyed learning and working together with the other children. Was the child happy most of the time? And what advise could they offer?

Also you can try talking to the absent parent, or the child's friends, and other relatives–and **remember not to speak negative about the child.** Tell them that you're only interested in helping the child to do well, and ask if they have any advice.

After talking with several people, you can determine who was a positive role model, and you might want to keep these people in your step-child's life.

How to Love Your Step-children

In order to love your step-children, you have to be mature in your thinking. Your own children have been trained to do things your way, but your step-children haven't.

Loving your step-children will require work. It begins with a decision to be responsible for the well-being of the child. You may never feel real love for this child, but you can receive a feeling of satisfaction and accomplishment once the child succeeds at the goals that you've set for him (or her). Let's talk about this briefly...

Children Are Our Secret Weapons

Children are from the Lord and the fruit of the womb is his reward (to you).

Ps. 127:3

Children are like guided-missiles. Once they're programmed, you can let them go, and they'll find the target, and explode.

Tell them that they were born to rule, and take over, by using their God-given talents, and the professional skills they learn in school. Tell them that the survival and protection of our people depends upon their education. That's why parents who live in poor neighborhoods must "protest" against having bad schools.

Starting today, you must teach your children to work together with people of their own race (just like other nationalities). Because if they don't, their own people can become weak, and easily go into slavery. Tell the children that people who don't work together, eventually stand together in free government-food lines.

You have a very special job to do, nurturing your re-marriage, and pro-gramming the step-children to become educated professionals who can take over the teaching jobs, the medical field, and create good laws for their peo-ple by going into politics.

Your step-children were born for the future survival of their family, to strengthen the community they live in, and for the good of all mankind. So find out what the children do well, and steer them in that direction.

Everything on Earth is Temporary

Your step-child might be a constant reminder that your spouse was in love with someone else before he (or she) married you. But again, mature think-ing is important if you're going to be a successful step-parent.

Everything on earth is temporary, therefore, the people who survive this life are the ones who learn to say *"Good-bye"* to the old, and *"Hello!"* to the new. You must accept the fact that it's okay to let go of old things (includ-ing people), and embrace what's new.

Eventually, your step-children will grow up and leave for college. So try to make the best of the few years they live with you. Also, it's wise to remem-ber that whatever affects your step-children, will also affect your new hus-band (or wife).

Pain is a Temporary Part of life

People die, move away, or get divorced, and in many cases, there's nothing we can do about it. We can choose to have a nervous break-down and allow ourselves to be institutionalized. Or, we can ask God to heal the pain.

You might think that you could never love anyone else again, but with God, all things are possible. You see, our Father knows that pain is a part of human life. That's why He promised to never leave us, nor forsake us. Pain is often the reason we invite Him into our lives, in the first place. And He gives us good things to take the pain away.

That's why He said in Psalms 91:14-16...

> *"Because (you) have set your love upon Me,*
> *therefore I will deliver (you);*
> *I will set (you) on high, because (you) have known my name.*
> *(You) shall call upon me, and I will answer (you);*
> *I will be with (you) in trouble;*
> *I will deliver (you) and honor (you)*
> *With long life I will satisfy (you), and show (you) My salvation."*

Being Jealous of Your Step-child can Destroy Your Marriage

It's easy to stay away from people who make you feel jealous, but when they live in your house, you need God's help, before it destroys your marriage:

> Your step-child is a constant reminder that your new spouse was in love with someone else before you.

> You might be afraid that your new spouse loves his own children more than you. Especially if he's always hugging, kissing, or defending them.

> Your new spouse is kind to his own children, but is always blaming and punishing your child.

> Family members who constantly compete with each other, will get jealous if one is more ambitious, and gets recognition, fame, or wealth.

Start by asking God for help! And because of your obedience, you can expect good results. —Also, thank Him for the promises He made to you and your spouse:

> *I belong to my lover, and his desire is for me*
>
> *(S.O.S. 7:10)*

Many waters cannot quench our love, neither can the floods drown it
(S.O.S. 8:7)

God has joined us together, and no one will separate us
(Mark 10:9)

Raising Your Children and
Your Step-Children Together

Sometimes there's a lot of anger between your children and your step children. And you must be the peacemaker, therapist, teacher, preacher, parent,
and friend. You also have to be the security guard who breaks up fights, and
calms tempers. Talking and lectures may seem endless, but it has its
rewards.

One of the rewards you have when the children leave home is the peace
from knowing that you did your best to rely upon God to raise those children.

You see, children need more than lessons about morality. They need real
tools to work with. For instance, each child deserves to live in a safe neighborhood where they can get an excellent education, medical care, and be
surrounded by positive role models.

Some children grow up, leave home, and accuse their parents of not prepar-
ing them for the business world. They might say that they weren't informed
about important and relevant issues pertaining to their survival and success.
So if you didn't teach them about financial planning, you can share your
knowledge with them as you learn.

You taught them God's word. You set an example before them. You told
them about life. You explained about your own mistakes, and you warned
them about the consequences of disobeying God.

Children Learn From the Adults Around them

Children learn their behavior from the environment they live in, and from the adults in their lives. For instance: manners and common courtesy, or cursing and fighting.

Children learn from their parents to read the Bible, to pray, and give offerings to God. Or they can learn to shoot guns, have sex, sell drugs, make drinks, and gossip.

The neighborhood you live in is very important because your children learn from their neighbors, and from the other kids at school, and from the business people around them.

How Children Feel
When Their Parents Get Divorced

When parents separate or divorce, they start dividing up the money, the children, and the furniture. They don't take their children's feelings into consideration, because they think that they're to young to know what's going on.

When parents separate or divorce, they should take their children's feelings into consideration, because children are people too. Their feelings do count, and we need to let them know that we care about their feelings. Why? Because in the future, our children will become someone else's husband or wife. And someday, they might face the same situation, and unless they've had a good example, they might react in the same manner in which they recall their parents reacted. Like throwing things, cursing, fighting, or even denouncing Christ.

A parent's job is to make a good impression on their kids, and to teach them how to live in this world. What we do now will affect our children for the rest of their lives. Unfortunately we can't press the rewind button, and erase what has already happened. But we can apologize to our kids, and make changes where needed.

Whose Fault is it?

Children didn't ask to be here, but in many cases, the parents didn't ask for them either. But once they're born, it becomes the parent's responsibility to provide for and protect them.

This is not a perfect world, and there are no perfect people because every one has disobeyed God at some point in their lives. And many people are still paying for the wrong choices they've made. But regardless of their mistakes, they have experienced God's mercy, forgiveness, wisdom, guidance, and faithfulness.

Some adult children don't care if their parents repent and ask for forgiveness, because they're going to blame them for everything that goes wrong in their lives anyway. On the other hand, when things go well, the parents wont receive any credit, but at least they'll get a break from the criticism. Your adult children know right from wrong, and they've made their own choices, and one day, they'll have to repent and ask God for forgiveness.

Most parents have raised their children the best way they could, sacrificing everything, including going without their own needs met. Perhaps a step-parent was needed to help raise the children. And maybe the step-parent didn't get along with the children, so you had to spend many years listening to them argue, and always being forced to choose sides. This is nobody's fault, it's just a part of raising step-children.

> *He who says he is in the light but hates his brother,*
> *is therefore in darkness even until now.*
>
> *1John 2:9 LMSA*

Living with Disrespectful Children

Some parents are exhausted from fighting and arguing with their teens. As a last resort, they think that if something bad would happen, the teen would learn a lesson.

But the Bible tells us not to set our hearts on their destruction. Instead, it tells us to chastise them. This means to correct them. And if God wants us to correct them, then He'll have to tell us what to do (when we ask Him).

> *Chasten your son while there is hope,*
> *And do not set your heart on his destruction.*
>
> *Prov. 19:18 NKJV*

Time-out is good for little kids, but when you have teenagers, they're not going to sit quietly in a corner for five minutes. They will talk back and see how much they can get away with. Some will curse their parents out, and even hit them. This leaves the parents exhausted and looking for answers.

Spanking Your Children

Forty years ago, it was okay to beat your kids with fists, belts, sticks, extension cords, and switches. Society expected parents to keep their children under control, and it was left up to the parents to decide how to do it, as long as they didn't kill them. And during that time, you never heard of teenagers going to jail, except for a few who made serious mistakes. But today, most teenagers have been inside of a police precinct.

It's a good thing that laws were made to prevent child abuse. But when good parents discipline their children, neighbors can call the police, or children can have their parents arrested for hitting them. And even after the investigation finds the parents not guilty of "child abuse" the case is still kept open for a number of years.

The Music, TV, and Fashion Industry should be Charged with Child Abuse

Parents have become exhausted looking for ways to discipline children who have been influenced by the music, TV, and fashion industry. These businesses (including video games) teach our children to be violent, disrespectful, and to break the law everyday. –So **shouldn't these businesses be charged with child abuse?!!**

We're not allowed to hit them, but a judge will quickly send them out-of-state to a prison where everyone in that town makes a living working there. Without your child, that town wouldn't have any money! And it doesn't stop there...

People can actually buy stock in different prisons; the more prisoners there are, the more money people make. And the things that prisoners make (like license plates and paintings) are being sold all over the world. So even though they get paid for working, there are businesses that take their money by selling them food, cigarettes, and other things. –It's an economy.

Don't Be Controlled by Fear

Even though the Bible says that the "rod of correction" drives foolishness from our children, the law says that we can't hit them.

Teenagers know when their parents are controlled by fear. So they'll stay out late, knowing that their parents will be so relieved when they get home. And instead of taking action, the exhausted parents will finally be able to lay down and get a good night's sleep.

As a result, some teenagers play loud music, and refuse to turn it down. After a while, the exhausted parents ignore the loud music. And when the disrespectful teen fights with a brother or sister, the exhausted parents just yell at them. Unfortunately, when the parents ignore the teen's bad behavior, this teaches the other children that acting bad is one way to get more attention. So when the other children who believe in following your rules see that there's no consequences for disobeying you, then they'll break the rules too.

A little yeast works through the whole batch of dough.

Gal. 5:9 NIV

As yeast causes bread to rise, one disrespectful child can cause the other children to become rebellious.

How to Help Your Teenager

Between working and raising children, a parent of an out-of-control teen can easily become exhausted and make the mistake of throwing him or her out of the house (into the street). But before you do that...

You have to realize that you no longer have proper supervision over your child. Your child simply doesn't listen to you anymore. Well, when this happens, you have to accept the fact that **there are millions of people who are qualified, and gifted to help your teenager.**

Cast out the scoffer, and
contention will leave;
Yes, strife and reproach will cease.

Prov. 22:10 NKJV

Before your teenager gets into serious trouble, you want to seek professional intervention. Start by asking your child's doctor for a referral to the mental health clinic. Once you're there, talk to a therapist or psychologist about a program where your teenager will be able to:

continue going to school
work
develop skills for self control

Enrolling your child in a good teenage program doesn't mean that you don't love him or her. It simply means that you understand that **your child can't live with you forever**, and you're helping him or her to:

> prepare for the adult world
> complete their education
> be more responsible
> learn to communicate properly
> be more appreciative

You should see these agencies as an extension of your good parenting skills. And as a result, you'll still be involved in your teen's life. And with the additional supervision, he (or she) will continue making progress with more academic choices, employment opportunities, and recreational activities.

Protecting Your Children
from being Killed by Gangs

With so many people losing their jobs today, the churches have to take on a new responsibility–our children! **It cost $5000 to bury a kid whose been shot or murdered by gangs, so why not take a portion of this money and hire a person who's anointed to run a Summer Youth Program**.

They can rent a large van (or maybe more) and take the kids to the beach (it's free). Drive them to the country to see farm animals, take them to the pool, set up video games, put on plays, talent shows, fashion shows, etc. This way our kids will learn valuable skills and stay out of trouble (because everyone will not have a summer job, or be able to afford an expensive two-week camp).

Please keep the church doors open so they can safely hang out together. You might have to take up another offering, but it's money well spent!

Jesus came to seek and to **SAVE** that which was lost. So once they're Saved spiritually, God wants us to Save them physically!

Arguing with Your Spouse

And if a man also strive for masteries (like in sports)
he is not crowned except he competed lawfully.

II Tim. 2:5

Don't let anyone (or anything) cause you to stop doing things God's way. Placing greater value on pleasing other people or having your own way, doesn't make the Father happy.

> **Warn them before God against quarreling** *about words;*
> *it is of no value, and only ruins those who listen.*
>
> *...**Do your best to present yourself to God** as one approved, a work-man who does not need to be ashamed and who correctly handles the word of truth.*
>
> *Avoid **godless chatter**, because those who indulge in it, will become more and more ungodly.*
>
> *II Tim. 2:14-16 NIV*

When the Holy Spirit prompts you to be quiet, stop arguing. This is to prevent other people (including little children) from hearing the wrong thing. Even if you win the argument, your words could cause serious damage to your relationship or to other people.

The Oldest Child

It's the oldest child who teaches us how to become good parents, and as a result, the younger children enjoy the benefits of our improved parenting skills.

Most parenting mistakes are made with the first child. As this child grows, he or she is usually expected to help with the younger children, and receives more household responsibilities than their friends. And in some cases, they receive no pay and a lot of criticism.

Ask Your Adult Children to Forgive You

So how do we ease the pain of a hurting child who now lives **inside** of a grown-up body. Or how do we erase the memories of their child abuse. And what do we do when "I'm sorry" isn't enough...?

The answer is to ask God to forgive you, and to give you an opportunity to have a loving relationship with that child.

If your adult son or daughter is experiencing difficulty as a result of the past, then go to them, and tell them the truth–you were wrong. After you have apologized, there is absolutely nothing else you can do to change the past.

> The one thing you can do is to be honest with your young adult and explain that you were young and without the Lord...
>
> Or, you were young in the Lord and had to mature in the ways of God. And you didn't mean to hurt him (or her).

If your older children are jealous because things are easier for their younger siblings, then explain to them how the Lord has made you a better person, and that's why you're able to recognize your mistakes, apologize, and change.

You can't go back and change the past. And more importantly, you must not allow guilt to hurt your present, or affect your future. **God knows that you are truly sorry.**

In order to live, you need to grow. And that involves forgiving others, and having them forgive you. In Mat. 18:22, Jesus said if you sin 490 times in one day, you should be forgiven by other believers. However, young people might not be so quick to forgive. But after you repent and "ASK" for their forgiveness, then it's up to them to forgive, or not to forgive. But it's good to know that your prayers are not hindered because you've been forgiven by God.

Your older children should be told that in order for a Christian to receive forgiveness from God, they must "forgive others."

All sin must be forgiven. And Jesus' blood provides that forgiveness—that washing of the soul, and that cleansing of the conscience. If He hadn't died in our place, we'd have to pay the penalty for our sins. But thanks to Him, we don't owe any punishment for sin, because His blood has paid our debt in full.

Prov. 31:28 is about a woman whose children grow up and praise her for the fine job she's done. Many mothers know this joy; but sadly, some mothers will not. But it's okay, as long as God has forgiven you.

Q. **I raised my children in church, and taught them about God. After high school, they all went to college, but only one graduated. Now they're selling drugs, prostituting, stripping, drinking, and cursing! Where did I go wrong?**

A. It's called economics! And it's real. Your adult children have bills to pay, and since they didn't go to college, they had to find a "hustle." This is a quick and easy way to make money on the streets.

Your adult children know right from wrong, because you've taught them. But after reading the chapter on "Prayer" you'll understand that no one in their right mind would reject Jesus' offer and later plunge into hell. So obviously, your children aren't in their right minds. And while it's true that you don't have power over your children's wills—**you do have power over the devil and demons.** You have power to bind him, and claim your children's deliverance and salvation. When you bind him, he has to stop blinding the eyes of your adult children so they can understand the gospel.

So rejoice, because all you have to do now is continue thanking God for their salvation. Remember, **God made an Agreement with you**, it's called a covenant. This means that He promised to keep His word. He didn't forsake David when he fought Goliath. All David had to do was obey God, and God did the rest. And that's what parents have to do—obey the Spirit of God.

Parents should help their adult children when the Holy Spirit leads them to. Other than that, parents should spend quality time with the Lord, and find out what He wants them to do with the rest of their lives.

Dealing With Death in the Family

Q. **God gave me the best husband in the world. But his mother died, and the next year his sister died. So now he gets depressed and stays up all night watching T.V.**

There are times when I need his attention, or I want to make love, but I refuse to bother him when he's thinking about them. It's been two years, and I'm frustrated because it seems that he's giving them more attention then me.

His mother and sister lived across the street from each other. And our house is right around the corner. But after the sister died, her husband moved away, and now there's two empty houses around the corner.

Since my husband's 80-year-old father lives in a nursing home, he has to manage his parent's empty house and their mail. So for the last two years, after work, he goes to his parent's house before coming home. His behavior frightens me, and I just want to move away from here and start our lives over.

A. Beloved, your answer is in "Saying" what the Bible says about your marriage. Why? Because there's a spiritual law that says, you will have whatever you say (Mark 11:23).

Secondly, you have to **do** what the Holy Spirit tells you to do for your husband. Because when you obey God, that's when He uses His power to change your circumstances.

Also, when you obey God, He gives you something that prevents you from **losing your mind,** or **having a heart attack**. It's called, "peace."

> *...the peace of God, which passes all understanding,*
> *shall keep your **hearts** and **minds** through Christ Jesus.*
>
> *Phil. 4:6*

So if your husband is in his right mind, you can be certain that God is with him, because Jesus said...

> *Peace I leave with you, **my peace I give to you**, ...let not your heart*
> *be troubled, neither let it be afraid.*
>
> *John 14:27*

Take this opportunity to sit quietly next to him, and if he needs to talk, listen to him (without offering any advice). His pain will decrease as time goes by, and he'll appreciate you for being there.

Q.   I just began the menopause because my period ended—and I'm a little scared.

**A.   **I'm sure you've heard so many things about this time in a woman's life. But if you do some research, you'll find that the women who experience severe problems during menopause are those who are nutritionally and physically in poor shape. Some of them never took vitamins, or drank water, or exercised.

Smart women prepare for this time of life by praying, exercising, eating right, drinking water, and taking supplements. Also they've developed a habit of visiting their doctor and dentist regularly. So when they go through the menopause, they have very few symptoms.

As for those who didn't prepare, it's not to late to **change to a healthy lifestyle**. You can start by getting information at your local health food store, or Christian book stores.

Q. **I believe in tithing, but my spouse doesn't. How do I avoid arguments regarding this?**

A. God is not in the business of breaking up marriages. So ask Him to give you your own money; then start tithing with the money He gives you.

God doesn't want you to love anyone or anything above Him. He wants first place. When He has first place in our lives, it's not hard to please Him.

Christians put God first, but in **different areas** of their lives. This is why you see one Christian prosper financially, one prosper in their marriage, another prosper in their health, and another prosper in their knowledge of the Bible.

Financial prosperity comes from giving money to God so He can get His work done–**and then expecting** Him to bless you to make more money—so you can continue giving.

The more you give, the more **you should expect God to do for you.**

Expect to receive money from (your job, promotions, increases, grants, sweepstakes, contests, gifts, services, contracts, favors, offerings, donations, etc...).

If you have a desire to give, or if you NEED something, the way to receive from God, is to GIVE Him something first. After you give Him your time, energy, or money, then ask Him to give you something back (but be specific—ask for the thing that you want!). This is what He wants you to do, and this is one reason why He sent **the Holy Spirit.** When it comes to making money, the Holy Spirit will tell you where to go, who to speak to, and what to say:

> *For He will not speak His own message [on His own authority];*
> *But He will tell (you)* **whatever He hears** *[from the Father;*
> **He will give the message that has been given to Him]**, *and*
> *He will announce and declare to you the things that are to come*
> *[that will happen in* **the future***].*
>
> *John 16:13 AMP*

Q.   How can I be sure that I am hearing from God?

A.   It's your responsibility to make sure that it's God that you're hearing from, and not the devil, or your own self. Whatever God tells you can be confirmed by His word. Just ask the Father to give you a scripture to confirm (or prove) that He has spoken.

When God speaks, His words agree with your spirit (not necessarily your feelings). However, you will feel uneasy if you refuse to do what He says.

THE REAL REASON FOR HAVING CHILDREN

When believers die, we must leave our Inheritance to our children. This includes our history, money, assets, property, and all of our earthly rewards and material possessions.

The time is over for Christians to die and leave their children with nothing. We must leave them everything we acquired with our faith while we were alive.

Remember, they also have the responsibility to win souls in their generation. There's no time for them to struggle for finances, or a place to live, or search for self-identification. Teach them who they are:

> Start by asking God to teach you how to think. Then be willing to sit under anointed and effective teachers who will instruct you how to use your faith and become a productive member of the Body of Christ.

Children must understand that **one of the jobs** of the body of Christ **collectively** is to work together to improve our lives.

No More Unemployment

Believe that God has already blessed your hands to create and to build. Believe that He will cause others to buy your products and pay for your services. –then get busy!

It's time to remove the negativity of the Entertainment Business by working together to create our own movies, plays, and theaters. We're able to televise our own music award ceremonies, and to applaud our own entertainment stars.

We offer the world wholesome family entertainment at their local movie theaters which are owned and operated by Christian entrepreneurs. Jesus said:

> **"...Do business until I come."**
> *Luke 19:13 NKJV*

Working Together

> *When he returned after having received the Kingdom,*
> *he ordered these bond servants to whom he had given the money*
> *to be called to him that he might know how much each one had*
> *made by* **"buying and selling."**
> *Luke 19:15*

Jesus wants us to put our money together to buy and sell real estate and land. He wants us to become landlords and rent out apartments and businesses. He wants us to invest in thousands of business projects (all over the world). Together we can prevent unemployment or homelessness among our brethren, and provide enough money to preach the gospel all over the world.

Christian Owned Banks!

> *...why did you not put* **my money in a bank,**
> *so that on my return, I might have collected it with interest?*
> *Luke 19:23 AMP*

When you deposit your money in the bank, large amounts become available for big companies to borrow. And after their newly-created businesses begin making money, they repay the loan (and interest). **Interest is the amount banks charge you for borrowing their money** (whether it's cash or their credit cards).

We can Work Together and create **our** own banks. Imagine loaning **our** money to big companies, and millions of people carrying **"God's Money"** credit cards, which enables Church-members to create hundreds of (money-making) businesses; like **Laundromats** and **SUPERMarkets**. --This is how God wants us to Think!

You see, Jesus wants the money He's given us to be put (together) in a bank, so Christians can make money by loaning their money to big companies (and to each other). But **Jesus won't be happy if we refuse to work together with** the (entire) Body of Christ.

> *...in you all the families of the earth shall be blessed.*
>
> *Gen.12:3*

God Works Miracles When You Obey Him

> *He who ...works miracles among you,*
> *does He do it by the works of the law,*
> *or by the hearing of faith*
>
> *Gal. 3:5*

When Abraham got ready to offer up Isaac as a sacrifice, God said, "Because you have obeyed me, I'm going to bless you!..." Well, God didn't bless Abraham alone. He also blessed Abraham's descendants. And one of Abraham's descendants is Jesus Christ. Therefore, every Christian who is in Christ, is also blessed along with Abraham.

> ***... if you are Christ's, then you are Abraham's seed,***
> *and heirs according to the promise.*
>
> *Gal. 3:29*

So God blessed Abraham, his descendants, and those who are in Jesus Christ. And to make sure that everyone can participate in this blessing, **here's my version** of what God said in Gal. 3:28.

> *"To me, there is no difference between the **Jews, or Africans,** or **Asians, or Europeans.** Because I am not prejudice."*
>
> *Gal. 3:28.*

Abraham's Children
are From Different Nationalities

Abraham's descendants are from different nationalities. Joseph's children were **half Egyptian**, and Jacob blessed (his grandsons) and called them by Abraham's name.

> *And to Joseph were born two sons ...whom Asenath (an **Egyptian** woman), the daughter of Poti-Pherah, priest of On, bore to him.*
>
> *Gen. 41:50 NKJV*

> *...Israel (Jacob) saw Joseph's sons, and said, "Who are these?"*
>
> *And Joseph said to his father, "They are my sons,*
> *whom God has given me in this place (**EGYPT**)."*
> *And he said, "Please bring them to me, and **I will bless them**."*
> *...Let my name be named upon them,*
> ***And the name of my fathers ABRAHAM***
> *and Isaac*
>
> *Gen. 48:8, 9, 16*

You Are Abraham's Seed

> ***...And if you are Christ's, then you are Abraham's seed,***
> *and heirs ...to the promise.*
>
> *Gal. 3:29*

Only those who obey God's voice are Abraham's descendants. So now it's time to get busy, and...

> **"...Do business until I come."**
>
> *Luke 19:13 NKJV*

Therefore, **GO AND WORK TOGETHER WITH YOUR BROTHERS**

AND SISTERS — and write children's books, make designer clothes, open restaurants, hotels, construction companies, transportation services, gas stations, supermarkets, private schools, giant Laundromats, dry cleaners, discount stores, etc...

Teach the 5-hour driving course and receive $45 per person. Imagine how much money you will make since every Christian driver must take it annually.

Abraham's Seed Works Together

Here's a few ideas that will create jobs.

Put your money together and help the women in your church:

> ...to buy sewing machines. And buy a building (or work from their homes) and begin sewing school uniforms, and sell them in our Christian-owned stores. Also, create daycare centers and private after-school programs in their homes. And don't forget beauty shops and house-cleaning services.

Put your money together and help the men in your church:

> ...to buy tow trucks for Christian Towing Services. Create private taxis and van services for our senior citizens, and services that will help people with snow removal, going to doctor appointments, and home improvements.

> I hope you're listening, because we need our own barber shops. And just think of the number of men who will be employed at our own SUPERmarkets, Laundromats, and dry cleaners.

> Oh yeah, and don't forget to create training programs where the men in your church can learn to cut grass, landscaping, and how to grow food (to sell).

Christian educational funds can train our young adults:

> ...to do construction work, and home improvements. They can learn to perm hair, provide faxing, copying, and typing services, and produce and sell merchandise like jewelry and clothes. And, oh yeah, **healthy** restaurants!

Put your money together and help the people in your church:

> Start home-based businesses. Home school moms can prepare students for the ELA and Math tests, Regents, SHAT, PSAT, and SAT tests.
>
> Help several couples in your church to prepare their homes for babysitting services, foster kids, and long-term senior care.

THE REAL PURPOSE FOR MARRIAGE

God Wants Children

Has not the Lord made them one?
In flesh and spirit they are his. And why one?
*Because **He was seeking Godly offspring.***

Mal. 2:15 NIV

God created marriage so we would have children. And He wants them raised to believe in His Powers; not in Santa Claus, Super heroes, or the tooth fairy.

Fairytales

It needs to be made clear that the real Super Hero is God, and that fairy-tales are just stories. Fairytales teach children that they're rewarded with love, marriage, and riches for believing in (and practicing) witchcraft, sorcery, black-magic, and spells. For instance, a fairy God mother will help them to marry a rich and handsome husband.

Comic Books

If you examine all of the imaginary power of the comic-book super heros, you'll agree that God is the only Super Hero who has **real powers.** He has healing power, money-making power, and life-giving power. He has marital power, fertility power, and parenting power. He can stop time, destroy entire armies, and bring people back to life. He can create new families and restore broken marriages. --Whatever you need, God will use His powers to help you if you follow His instructions.

He wants us to tell our children what He said concerning them, "...who they are, what belongs to them, and what they can do." He wants them to know how to think, how to speak, and how to act in the Kingdom of God. He wants them successful, because **they are tomorrow's church.**

Created To Rule

God wants a world of faith-filled BELIEVERS (men, women, and children) **to use their God-given imagination and gifts** to create jobs, businesses and services. He wants you to **be the head. The boss. The employer.**

> *This is what the Lord says to his anointed,*
> *...whose right hand I take hold of*
> ***to subdue nations before him***
> *and to strip kings of their armor,*
> *to open doors before him (for you to enter in, and)*
> ***so that gates will not be shut****:*
>
> *Isa. 45:1*

It's time for the BODY OF CHRIST to EDUCATE OUR CHILDREN in every industry; politics, business, manufacturing, education, medicine, agriculture, marine life, aero-space, environmental, and every socio-economic area of life.

God's Dream

This is God's dream. Faith-filled **BELIEVERS owning and operating all the resources of His earth.** This way, we'll have enough money to finance the gospel, feed the hungry, clothe the naked, heal the sick, and visit those in prison. When Jesus returns for His Glorious church, He'll find us effectively evangelizing the world. This is how our children must be trained to think.

Teach them that we no longer live by the same rules and principles of the world's system (or the kingdom of darkness). Yes, we obey the laws of the land; but if these laws harm or endanger our lives and freedom, then collectively, we must change the laws.

Freedom to worship our God is essential to our peace. Fulfilling our purpose and pleasing our Father is essential to our well-being.

You must teach your children that the reason God has so many different churches is so that they can work together.

WORK TOGETHER
TO FINISH GOD'S WORK

We must teach our children to:

> **WORK TOGETHER** with OTHER BELIEVERS
> (people who believe that Jesus' words are true);
>
> **WORK TOGETHER** with other denominations,
> and be led by the Holy Spirit TO BUILD, and
> TO CREATE JOBS. (Gen. 1:26)

Tell them that we must **TRUST THE CHRIST IN ONE ANOTHER**.
We must learn to follow the voice of the Holy Spirit. We must learn to identify His voice, so we can obey Him, and succeed in life. Gen. 1:28 says:

> *And God BLESSED them... (**HOW?**)*
> *He commanded them to be fruitful,*
> *multiply, and replenish (re-fill) the EARTH...*

Keep reading to find out why He wanted SO MANY God-blessed people on the earth:

Q. Where in the Bible did God command us to sit peacefully among sinners and let them rule over us?

Where did He say, "Let them hire and fire you?"
Where did He say, "Let them feed you?
Where did He say, "Let failing schools teach your children?"

Q.   Who is blessed by God; sinners or saints?

A.   At one time, Adam and Eve were like God, without sin. (They had not sinned yet).

And God commanded them to multiply and to fill (replenish) the earth with people who were like them—good people.

The Well-Being of the Body of Christ

Subduing the earth means to **conquer it and bring it into subjection to the will of God**. This is done by submitting ourselves to God. Then following His Holy Spirit as He guides us into fulfilling our earthly assignments.

Subduing the earth means to overpower evil with good. For some Christians, it means to allow the Holy Spirit to (legally) guide them into politics and governmental jobs. For others, it might mean to own and operate their own Christian schools.

To conquer means to do good everywhere we see evil. Conquer hunger with food. Conquer sickness with prayer and medicine. Conquer nakedness with clothes. And conquer homelessness with shelter.

Although we all have different gifts, subduing the earth means that each and every Christian must become a willing participant in the well-being of the Body of Christ.

> *It was he (Jesus) who gave some to be _apostles_,*
> *some to be _prophets_, some to be _evangelists_, and*
> *some to be _pastors_ and _teachers_, to*

PREPARE GOD'S PEOPLE FOR WORKS OF SERVICE, *(so that the body of Christ may be built up)*
UNTIL WE ALL REACH UNITY *in the faith and in the knowledge of the Son of God and*
BECOME MATURE, *attaining to the whole measure of the fullness of Christ.*

Eph. 4:11-13

It is our responsibility to evangelize the earth with the Gospel of Jesus Christ. Some of us are called to teach and preach. While the others are called to make sure that the earth is evangelized by sending money to whomever God tells us to. Those called to the five-fold ministry should not have to raise the money too. That is what the rest of the Body of Christ is suppose to do.

From him (Christ) the whole body,
JOINED AND HELD TOGETHER

by every SUPPORTING ligament
(each person doing his/her job),

grows and BUILDS ITSELF UP in love,
AS EACH PART DOES ITS WORK.

Eph. 4:16

Subdue means to flood the earth with good deeds. **Every Christian working, creating, developing, inventing, participating, encouraging, supporting, caring, and loving, with one purpose in mind; being a blessing to the ever-growing family of God.**

*Then **WE WILL NO LONGER BE INFANTS**, tossed back and forth by the waves, and blown here and there by every wind of teaching and by the cunning and craftiness of men in their deceitful scheming.*

Eph. 4:14 NIV

God does not want us to be like infants; **powerless to change our lives and the lives of our children.**

Unless you are willing to fulfill God's will for your life, you will always be told where to live, and what you can have.

God wants us to become MATURE, and begin thinking, acting, and speaking like Jesus. When it comes to marriage and starting a family, your prosperity and health are involved. So it's vital that you let God choose who you will marry. He already knows who will work well with you, and who wont.

THE REAL REASON FOR MONEY

Seed, Time, and Harvest
(explained easily)

People who live in big cities eat their fruit and throw away the seeds. They don't expect to get anything back. In fact, they just want the garbage man to take them away with the rest of the trash.

But a farmer's survival depends on throwing the seeds in the ground and **expecting to get something back.**

God Spoke Your Needs into Existence

> *Thus the heavens and the earth were finished, and **all the host of them,** And on the seventh day God ended His work which He had done; and He rested on the seventh day from ALL His work which He had done.*
>
> *Gen. 2:1-2 AMP*

In six days, **God created everything that you could possibly want.** But everything was in the form of a *seed.* Let's talk about *a seed* for a moment:

> In their bodies, Adam and Eve carried the seeds for the next generation. And to make sure that the next generation would eat, God put seeds into every fruit and vegetable; also into the animals, birds, and fish. Therefore, as long as the earth remains, babies will be born, and there will be food for them to eat.

Here's another example:

> In the beginning, God created a few orange trees. And those trees produced oranges for the people who lived during that time period. And today, we're still enjoying oranges because of the abundance of seeds.

A billion years ago, God made sure we would have food to eat today. But what about a new house to live in, or a new car to drive to work?

Before we were born, God had already created our new houses, cars, and businesses. First, He made sure all of the materials were in the earth. And at the right time, certain people were given the knowledge to use the materials to make houses and cars.

So how do we get our new houses and cars? –This is where God comes in. First, He said to "ask" Him! And after we ask, then He'll tell us where to go, what to say, and what to do.

> *...your Father knows the things you have need*
> *of before you **ask** Him.*
>
> *Mat 6:8*

> *...Whatsoever ye shall **ask** the Father*
> *in my name, he will give it to you...*
>
> ***ask**, and ye shall receive,*
> *that your joy may be full.*
>
> *John 16:23, 24*

> *...your Father who is in heaven give good things*
> *to those who **ask** Him!*
>
> *Mat. 7:11 NKJV*

> *...him who is able to do exceeding, abundantly,*
> *above all that we **ASK** or THINK*
>
> *Eph. 3:20*

Now to get a better understanding, let's take another example:

> If you want a new car, **ask God**, and He'll tell you what you have to do.
>
> He might ask you to give something, or do something, or say something, or go somewhere. You see, there's a seed called "*obedience*." And you'll have to obey God's instructions in order to get the new car.

You already know what seed to plant to get watermelons, but **you don't know what to do to get a new house**, a new kidney, or a new job.

Strange Seeds

As I said before, When God rested on the seventh day, He had already created everything you need to survive on the earth —a house, a car, a business, etc...

But since you weren't born yet, He saved them for you in the form of a "seed." As a result, He's the only one who knows what seed would cause you to get these things.

So if He tells you to give money, then give it. Because although it might look like money to you, God sees it as a seed. If He tells you to give away jewelry, it might look like you're giving away something precious. But God see's your "obedience" as a seed. And (giving) or planting these seeds where He tells you, will produce the things you need.

Plant Seeds Everyday

Everyday you give your time, energy, and money towards getting the things you want:

1. If you want a paycheck, you have to work for two weeks.

2. If you want a driver's licence, you have to study and practice.

3. If you want a hot meal, you have to shop for it, and then cook.

4. If you want clean clothes, you have to wash and iron them.

But there's some things only God can get for you. And if you're going to get anything from Him, you're going to have to give your time, energy, and money.

But there's a few Christians who think that God will give them things for free...

Expect to Receive Something Back

Another mistake that Christians make is that they give offerings, but they don't expect anything back. And when they don't receive anything from God, then they complain.

The reason why some Christians don't receive anything back after they give an offering, is because they don't understand that it's a spiritual law. The law says in Luke 6:38...

If you give something to God, then He'll make men give you more than what you gave.

Some Christians think that their jobs are finished after they give away their tithes and offerings, and continue being morally good. But God said to give AND to expect something back. So they're actually sinning by not obeying Him and not expecting something back that can be used for promoting the gospel.

After we have obeyed God by giving (a certain amount of money, or jewelry, or free help, etc...) He told us to expect to receive something back. In this scripture, He gave us instructions on how to expect to receive things from people....

"I have given AND (now other people give) to me
Good measure, pressed down, shaken together,

and running over, **people always give me (money, jewelry,
new clothes, cars, houses, services, and favor—all the time)."**

Luke 6:38

This is a spiritual law! –You're suppose to expect God to make people do things for you.

Oral Roberts once said that God told us (7 times) in Luke 6:38 to receive something back. Therefore, **always expect to get a whole lot, pressed down, shaken together, exceedingly, abundantly, more than you could ever ask or think.**

Expect big favors from other people. When someone says, "No!" it means that you've spoken to the wrong person–keep asking, and someone will tell you, "Yes!"

Words are Seeds, too

Each day is like an acre of soil. So the first thing in the morning, Christians should plant something in that dirt; if not, then satan will. He'll plant weeds and problems that will spring up throughout the day.

Every morning, they can choose to have a good day by (planting) or speaking "God's words" concerning their day.

> *..but while men slept, his enemy came and sowed tares (weeds) among the wheat and went his way.*

Mat. 13:25

God Doesn't Give Anything Away for Free

The law says that God will not give you something for free! You have to give Him something first (like the boy who gave Jesus the two fish and five loaves). So if you want to have more than the average lifestyle, you have to

give offerings – **ask** for what you want – **obey** (or follow His instructions) – and **expect** Him to give you what you asked for.

The Only Reason You're Suppose to Give– is so You Can Get Something Back

*Give, and **it shall be given** unto you...*

Luke 6:38

God would never be able to get His work done with a whole bunch of poor people. So He created a way for us to prosper financially. And after we have given, or finished the work He told us to do, then we can talk to Him like this:

> Father, I have obeyed your instructions, and given; and now the new car and the other things I asked you for have been given to me, in a good measure, that's pressed down, shaken together, and running over. Thank you for inspiring people to give me things all the time!

You see, the only reason you give something to God is so that He'll give you something back. And as a result, you'll have more than enough to help finance the gospel. Look at Phil. 4:15 NKJV...

> *...no church shared with me concerning*
> *"**giving and receiving**," but you only.*

You know that God is the only one who can help you. And you know that He created "**Giving and Receiving**" so you and your family can prosper financially. And everything He gives you, will help you to be more effective in assisting Him in the ministry.

> *He that has pity on the poor, lends to the Lord;*
> *and that which he has given, will he pay him again.*

Prov. 19:17

Proof that God Gives

When you asked God for a used car to drive for the next ten years, He gave it to you. When you asked Him for shoes to wear on the train for the next five years, He gave them to you. When you believed Him to stay healthy by taking medicine for the rest of your life, He granted your desire. –so why don't you just ask Him for what you really want.

What to do While You're Waiting

It might take a little while before you actually see changes in your circumstances. But be patient, and keep thanking God that **you already have the things you asked for**. Continue to obey Him, and never throw away your confidence in God.

> *After you have done the will of God,*
> *you will receive the promise*

1 John 5:14-15 says that God hears you every time you pray, and that **your request has been granted**.

So after you've done what He said to do, or (given what He said to give) then **continue praising Him**, and thanking Him that you already have the thing you asked for.

How to Get Your Bills Paid

When you use the Name of Jesus, it carries the full weight of Heaven. God honors the Name of His Son, and trillions of angels stand at attention, ready to work on your behalf. Even demons obey you when you command them to do something, **In the Name of Jesus!**

Jesus told you the truth when He said:

*Whatsoever ye shall ask the Father **in my name**, he will give it to you*
John 16:23

*...ask, and ye shall receive, **that your joy may be full***
(vs. 16)

Your joy is not full if your children are sick, or if you're bills are not paid. So, if you believe that Jesus didn't lie to you, then pray. (But make sure you're not living in open rebellion, or in disobedience to God. Because if you are, then the prayer wont work). But if you're doing what He told you to do, then expect the money to come!

Father:

Your Word says in Phil. 4:19. *"My God shall supply all your need according to his riches in glory by Christ Jesus."*

Your Word says that You are rich, and that you will supply all of my needs. (This bill is a need).

Your Word says in Mark 11:24**,** *"Therefore I say unto you, What things soever you desire, when ye pray, believe that ye receive them and ye shall have them.*

Therefore, I am asking you for $642.20 for my water bill, which is both, a need and a desire. And according to your instructions, I believe I already have the $642.20.

Now, Praise Him:

Father,

I thank you that you always hear me when I pray. (1 John 5:14) And, I thank you that I already have the money for my water bill. You said, *"...believe you **receive it**, and you shall have it."* So I **receive it!**

Now deal with the demon of doubt and unbelief whose job is to steal your money, your health, your family, and your faith in God!

> Listen devil, it is written in Mat. 18:18, *"Whatsoever I shall bind on earth, shall be bound in heaven..."* Therefore, I bind you, and I break your power, and I command you to take your hands off of my money.

Remember, you can break his power, and **command him to take his hands off of your money**, because you have been given more power than his (little suggestive) power. And nothing he does will harm you!

> *Behold, I give to you power to walk on serpents and scorpions, and **over** all the power of the enemy: and nothing shall by any means hurt you.*
>
> *...in this rejoice not, that the spirits are subject unto you; but rather rejoice, because your names are written in heaven.*
> *Lk 10:19, 20*
>
> *He called his twelve disciples together, and gave them power and authority over **all devils***
> *Luke 9:1*

Remember, God hears you when you pray the first time. He always hears you (1 John 5:14). So the next step is to follow His instructions.

And beloved, **somehow the money comes!** It comes from so many unexpected sources. And at the end of the month, when you add up all of the money you received, you'll see that He gave it to you. —Just make sure you use it for your bills.

When you pray (believing that God has already given you the money) and then follow the instructions that the Holy Spirit gives you for getting your bills paid, that's when the money will come.

Financial Gain

Your reason for living is to help God save people from the fires of hell. And He'll stop at nothing to help them. He'll even ask for your help.

He might ask you to preach, or to teach, or to give some money. When you give, your financial support enables His Gospel to be taught. As a result, people are saved. And your reward will be that God will keep His promise.

> *Give–AND— men will pour into your lap...*
> *Luke 6:38*

Because you gave what God told you to give, He said to expect people to give you money, food, clothes, excellent cars, expensive jewelry, debt-free houses, Wills, estates, favor, mercy, discounts, computers, furniture, etc. God wants you to **expect something back** each time you give. You might need money, or have a desire for something else, but whatever it is, He promised that—if you follow His instructions—all of your **needs** will be supplied (Phil. 4:19).

God has already granted, or said, "Yes!" to your desires. But you'll have to follow His instructions in order to receive them. For instance, He might tell you to return to school, or apply for a certain job, or to ask a certain person for the amount you need.

The Right Relationship

God said, *"Ask, and it shall be given."* This means that if you ask Him, then He'll tell you how to get the things you want.

He said, *"...acknowledge me in all your ways, and I'll direct your path."* God is saying that He will lead you every step of the way.

He also said, *"Whatever you desire, when you talk to me, If you believe that I already have it for you, then you will get it! Mark 11:24*

The only reason you go to God is because you believe that He is real. And the reason you talk to Him is because you believe that He always hears and answers you.

Well, you see, this is the kind of relationship God is looking for. And the only reason He's listening and talking to you is because He wants something from you, too... He wants people to be saved!

And if you'll do the things He asks you to do, then He will use His power to give you the things you ask Him for. As you can see, this relationship is based on **both of you** talking, listening, and doing what the other one asks.

Honoring God With the First Fruits

Retiring on Social Security alone, is not God's Will. If it was, He wouldn't have given us Prov. 3:9-10:

> *Honor the Lord with your wealth,*
> *and with **the first fruits of all your increase***
> *So shall thy barns* (bank accounts) *be filled with plenty,*
> *and your wine presses shall burst out with new wine.*
> *(You'll always have something to sell and make money with).*

Why does God want the first fruits? Because it proves that you love Him the most. You see, **when you receive money, the first person you think about is the one you love the most**. This person will receive money (or gifts) from you first.

This is a spiritual law. You see, God has exalted His word above His own name. And He has sworn by His own name that His word will accomplish what it was sent to do. And He watches over His word to perform it.

God said to honor Him **first** with your tithes and offerings, and He'll cause you to have a surplus of prosperity.

Where Extra Money Comes From

God promised that those who *"give"* whatever He tells them to give, would have a surplus of prosperity. This means enough money to pay your bills, and buy the things you want, and save some, and still be able to support the ministry.

Since this money wont fall from the sky, He told us where it will come from:

> *...the Lord shall make **you** have a surplus of prosperity,*
> *through the fruit of **your body** (your children),*
> *of **your livestock** (stocks, mutual funds, and investments)*
> *and of **your ground** (real estate),*
> *in the land which the Lord swore to your fathers to give you.*

God will bless **your children** with special money-making gifts. They will get recording contracts, modeling jobs, parts in movies, win contests, etc.

He'll cause your stocks, bonds, and mutual funds to increase.

But before large sums of money come to you, God will make sure that you learn about investing, because He wants your money to grow. You don't have to be a stockbroker, because the Holy Spirit will tell you which **stocks** to invest in (and when to sell them). And because you're a "giver," God will cause your dividends to increase.

You'll own your own house, and when you move, you'll either sell it, or rent it. In addition to that, you might inherit other houses. This is how money comes through **real estate**.

> *The Lord shall open to you His good treasury, the heavens,*
> *...to bless ALL the work of **your hands**...*
> > *Duet 28:11-12 AMP*

God promises to give you a surplus of prosperity from the things you create with your hands. This means that He'll give you books to write, or the words for new songs, or ideas for new inventions, or He'll direct you to a new career.

Expect Something Back

God told us to expect to receive something back when we give tithes and offerings:

> *He who has pity on the poor, lends to the Lord,*
> *And **that which he has given** He will repay to him*
>
> *Prov. 19:17 AMP*

In order to receive something, you have to **give** something.

> ***Give**, and it will be given to you...*
>
> *Luke 6:38*

And this is how God will repay you:

> *Good measure,*
> *pressed down,*
> *shaken together,*
> *and running over,*

This is a spiritual law—after you've obeyed God's instructions, and given the exact amount He told you (to a person or an organization) then the favor, money, and information that you need...

> *will be put into your bosom.*

You have to **believe that other people will obey God (just like you did)** and will give you the things you need.

> *...with the measure that you use,*
> *it will be measured back to you."*
>
> *Luke 6:38 NKJV*

How to Love God

Loving God has nothing to do with hugs, and kisses. Instead, God wants us to obey Him. Therefore, loving God is simply obeying His **"written"** and **"spoken"** word.

> *Love the Lord your God with **all your heart**
> and with **all your soul,** and with **all your mind**.*
> *Mat. 22:37 NIV*

Jesus loved God so much that He obeyed Him, and came to earth, and told us what God wanted us to know. Here's my version of what He said:

> *This is how we are to love God:*
> *...obey His commandments [because]*
> *...his commandments are not difficult.*
> *1 John 5:3*

When we're instructed to give, it's because God wants to carry out His promise of Luke 6:38 to someone. And after we give, we're suppose to **look for God to give us something back!** Why? Because we have needs too.

After we've done what God told us to do, we can talk to Him with confidence. For example:

> *"Father, I thank you for giving me a new house, because I've done everything you've asked me to do." Amen.*

Extra Money Comes From God

Even in the Old Testament, God promised to bless His people. Here's my version of Duet. 28:1-6...

> *If you will (seriously) **listen** to the voice of the Lord your God, (and*

make sure you do everything I tell you to do)
Which I command you (to do) each day, the Lord your God will set
you high above all the nations of the earth.

And all these blessings shall come upon you and overtake you
if you (obey) the voice of the Lord your God...   Blessed shall you
be in the city, ...and in the field, ...and in your body, ...when you
come in, and when you go out...

Duet 28:1-6

God will give you specific instructions. And if you do them, He'll cause your business to grow. If you take His voice seriously, you'll succeed at whatever you're doing. For example, when a farmer prays, and God tells him what to plant, once the seeds are planted in the ground, the farmer looks for God to keep His promise, and make it rain, ...and make it grow!

God Has a Treasury!

*The Lord shall open to you His good **treasury**, the heavens,*
to give the rain of your land in its season
and to bless ALL the work of your hands;

Duet. 28:12 AMP

Beloved, God has a treasury! This is a department in the Kingdom of God where money and valuable objects are kept until they're given to us. And this is the way we get things from His treasury:

...no church shared with me concerning
***Giving** and **Receiving**, but you only.*

...you sent aid once and again for my necessities.

*...fruit that abounds to **Your Account**.*

Phil. 4:15, 16, 17 NKJV

The words "**Giving**," "**Receiving**," and "**Your Account**" tells you that God has kept a record of every dollar you've given. In return, He promised to supply everything you need... You see, God is rich, and if He bought you everything you asked for, He still wouldn't be broke!

> ...*God will supply all of your needs*
> *according to His riches in glory*
> *(**which He promised**) through Jesus Christ.*
>
> *Phil. 4:19*

Of course money doesn't fall from the sky. Here's how it works: When someone has a need, God will tell you how much to give, and where to send the offering to.

And when you have a need, He'll either give you instructions on what to do, where to go, and what to say. Or, He'll instruct someone else to give it to you.

God will bless anyone who listens to His voice and does what He says. These are the instructions for winners. And it's never to late to begin.

Q. **When my husband gets paid, he comes home broke because he looses all of his money gambling. So he sells drugs to pay the bills.**

   I'm a Christian, and I've warned him that this illegal activity will send him to prison. But he continues to sell drugs. Does God want me to stay with him, even though he's putting me and the children in danger?

A. Sinners sin, because that's what they do. And it's not easy to leave someone you love just because they've sinned. They're separated from God, that's why they endanger the mental, physical, and emotional well-being of others.

If you and your children are in danger because of the physical violence that's associated with drug dealing, you need to pray for a safe place to live.

Since Christians can approach the ***Throne of Grace with confidence,*** and ***receive mercy*** and ***find help*** in their time of need, you can pray for the salvation of your family (Heb. 4:16).

> *The Lord is not slow in keeping his promise,*
> *as some understand slowness.*
> *He is patient with you,*
> ***not wanting anyone to perish,***
> *but everyone to come to repentance.*
>
> *2 Pet. 3:9 NIV*

God is Interested in Your Family

God is interested in the salvation of your family. The proof is that He gave His only son as full payment for each one of their sins.   (John 3:16)

Since faith works by love—and you love your family—then your prayers for money will be heard, and **your expectations will be granted.** Why? Because God said:

> *Whatever you ask for in prayer,*
> *(You have to first) believe that I will give it to you*
> *and* then ***you will get it.***
>
> *Mark 11:24*

We're Christians, and we're suppose to believe what God says. He said in Duet. 28:12 that He has blessed all the works of our hands. And in Luke 6:38 **God said that we're suppose to give money, and expect other people to give it back to us.** Why? Because in the Kingdom of God, the Father rules. And these are the rules He set up for us to win financially. So if you want to win (in this life) you'll have to play by His rules.

> *Each man should give* (God wants us to give)
> *what he has decided to give in his heart*
> *not grudgingly (or out of necessity;* **thinking it's something that**
> **he has to do, and unsure if God will give him anything back)**

for God loves a cheerful giver (one who knows he will get
something back).

2 Cor. 9:7

God wants to give us money, but first we must have **a full understanding**
of our financial covenant.

And God is able (He's willing to use His power)
to make all grace (every earthly blessing)
abound to you (happen in your life to satisfy all of your needs)
so that you will always have more than enough (you will
always have the things you need; like bill payments,
 grocery money, clothing, or whatever you need.)
you will abound in every good work (and be able to help
other people).

(Vs. 8)

As it is written:
*He has scattered abroad his **gifts to the poor;***

(Vs. 9)

Giving to God, ensures your survival:

*Now he who **supplies***
*seed to the sower **and bread** for food,*
*will also **supply***
***and increase** your store of seed*
***and will enlarge** the harvest of your righteousness*

(Vs. 10)

The more you give what God tells you to give, the more He'll increase your
supply. This transaction will eventually make you financially independent.

*You will be **made rich** in every way*
*so that you can **be generous** on every occasion,*

God wants you to be rich, because when you give to other people, they will
lift up their voices with praise and give Him all of the glory.

*...**This service** that you perform is*
*not only **supplying the needs of God's people,***
*but is **also overflowing in many expressions of thanks to God.***
2 Cor. 9-12 NIV

The Real Reason For Money

...the Son of Man came to seek and to save sinners.
Luke 19:10

What else is money for? It's certainly not to pay the world to dominate and control you and your children!

Our money is supposed to be used to help each other to obtain licenses, and get involved in real estate, and many other money making opportunities. Look around your community. Then go to your church and ask, "How can we make money to help our community? Then pray about it. Eventually, the members of your church will begin working, and living better than they've ever dreamed of.

Learn how to Work Together with the body of Christ, and learn how to multiply your money. This way, there will be money left over for the next generation of Christians to win souls. (see "usgodpower" on Youtube).

Are you starting to get the picture of why you were assigned to your spouse and the real reason for marriage?

Are you beginning to understand that each member of the body of Christ has an assignment for the well-being of the entire body. **Each and every member is needed.**

Securing Our Children's Future

All children need "**recognition**," "**opportunity**," "**belonging**," and "**security**."

They want to be seen, so let them usher in church. They want an opportunity to be make a contribution, so create small (paid) jobs for them in the church and in the community. They want to belong to a group, so let them wear uniforms and sing on the choir; or join the Junior Executive Club.

If you don't have these programs or clubs, please create them. Someone in your church is successful, knowledgeable, and skilled, and can teach the children about business.

Finally, all children need to feel safe. So ask God to bless you to live in a safe neighborhood, with the best schools, and where the adults serve as role models. If you're not able to move, then join a local community-based organization that's working towards making your neighborhood better.

It's Time to Create
A "Safe" Culture

The body of Christ must work together to ensure that all children, teens, and seniors, can feel safe in their schools, at home, or walking down the street.

It is our job, as believers, to restore our communities back to a place where our families feel safe.

Dealing With Drug Dealers

Drug dealers have the right to gamble with their freedom if they choose to sell drugs. And addicts have the right to gamble with their lives if they choose to buy and use drugs. However, the other citizens of the community have the right to remain drug free, and live in a safe environment.

> *...**the Lord will drive out** all these nations from before you, and you will dispossess **greater and mightier** nations than yourselves.*
>
> *Duet. 11:23*

We don't want our children going to drug dealers or asking other people for jobs as though Christ has to beg, borrow, and plead.

Instead of tearing each other down, our children will form Christian alliances and explore science, technology, and other business ventures together.

We must teach our children to trust the Christ in each other, and appreciate the gifts that He's placed in each one of us. We must learn to work together, and depend on one another, and support each other's ideas.

We do support one another. We do appreciate, prize, value, esteem, and honor, one another. Why? Because Christ lives in each of us.

We **do not support** any negative (or poverty-minded) ideas of ourselves, our country, our families, our children, our grandchildren, our employment, or our financial well-being.

We are the children of a KING, which makes us Princes and Princesses.

We are motivated, educated, and well-informed about God's Will. His Will is written in His Word! We are filled with God's wisdom, understanding and knowledge. We are filled with the nature of God, washed clean in the Blood of Jesus; forgiven, Blessed to Prosper, and Commanded by God to be in control.

From Slavery to Prosperity

After God saved the Jews from the Holocaust, He blessed them to work together to prosper on earth. And after God delivered the African-Americans from Slavery, He blessed them to Work Together, too!

We are hungry for change, motivated to act, and willing to work together. We're flexible enough to learn, easy to train, quick to pray, willing and obedient, and ready to prosper.

When the righteous rule, the people rejoice, so it's time for you to rule.

There is a System that God uses to bless you and your children:

> *I will surely bless you, and make your descendants*
> *as numerous as the stars in the sky and as the sand*
> *on the seashore.*
>
> *Your descendants will **TAKE***
> ***POSSESSION OF THE CITIES OF THEIR ENEMIES***
> *and through your offspring all nations on earth will be*
> *blessed, because you have obeyed me.*
>
> *Gen. 22:17-18 NIV*

The only reason anyone would have as many children as the sand on the seashore, is because **THEY'VE GOT A JOB TO DO TOGETHER...** *(which is) to possess the gates of their enemies.*

> God said that Christians would live in cities where the dominant group of people don't like them.
>
> He said that all of your children, working together, would take control over all the **CITIES** in the world (where the people who live and work there don't like them).
>
> Now if the people who control and operate the city love your descendants, then this scripture is not about you. But if they don't like you, and they don't like your children, then get ready...
>
> *... and THROUGH YOUR OFFSPRING **all nations on earth** will be blessed, because you have obeyed me.*
>
> *Gen. 22:18 NIV*

God does not want us to depend on the world, its system, and its mercy to survive. Instead, He wants us to do what Abraham did—And that's to do exactly what God tells us to.

Jesus became poor in our place, so that we can become rich. He also removed the curse (of sin and death) so we could have the same blessings that Abraham enjoyed. He went through a lot for us to become rich, because He wants His good news to be preached all over the world. That's why He anointed some people to preach—and gave the rest money-making talents, abilities, and skills that will enable the gospel to be preached in churches, on radio, television, movies, DVD's, CD's, and the world wide web.

We're all connected to these ministries; therefore, we all have a part to play in winning souls (in our generation). And with our money, we can make sure that our children will be able to win souls in the future.

The Holy Spirit wants to lead you into your God-given assignment in this life. You wont accomplish anything by sitting there wondering "What's God's plan for my life?" You have to ask Him. Then the Holy Spirit will be more than happy to show you what you're suppose to be doing.

Why Christians Must Be the Head

God wants you to work together with other believers to transfer the CASH into your hands. And He'll show you how:

    a. To please God (Heb. 11:6)
    b. To do work that you love (Ecc. 5:19);
    c. To use your talents and skills to change our society (Mat. 5:14-16)
    d. To build a society with God's ideas and activities (Eph. 5:1)
    e. To solve real problems, for real people (Gal. 6:10)
    f. To Finance the gospel (2 Cor. 9:12-14)
    g. To have compassion on the fatherless and widows (James 1:27)
    h. To educate, protect, and provide for your own (2 Tim. 5:3)
    I. To have mercy and exercise justice as God would (Micah 6:8)

j.   To fulfill your assignment of Gen. 1:28
k.   To enjoy your life (Ecc. 5:19)
l.   To be in good health (III John 2)
m.   To leave an inheritance for your grandchildren (Prov. 13:22)

Dominion

Let's look at Gen. 1:28 again:

> ...*replenish the earth,*
> *and SUBDUE IT; (bring it under our control) and*
> *HAVE DOMINION OVER*
> *the fish of the sea,*
> *the fowl of the air, and*
> *EVERY LIVING THING THAT MOVES ON THE EARTH*

If we don't do it — satan will.

Q.   **What does God want us to have dominion over**?

A.   First let's define Dominion:

For Christians, Dominion is a good word. It means having the Power or right of governing and controlling for the purpose of doing good things for people and the earth. It means **being in a position of authority.** It means ruling with the intentions of doing good. It means taking over the territory where people are hurting or mourning so you can bring comfort, peace, and joy.

Does God want Christians to run for political offices?
Does God want Christians to do good and make people happy?
Does God want Christians to exercise fairness, justice, and equity to all men? — Of course.

PRAYER

Prayer is a Christian's Life! And it's one of the easiest things to do. Without it God couldn't hear your problems and give you the answers.

Who Do We Pray To

Jesus said to **pray to God**, our Heavenly Father.

> *Whatever you ask **THE FATHER** in my name, He will give it to you.*

And God requires that you pray in the name of His son. Because He honors the name of His son.

> *For the Father judges no one, but has committed all judgment to the Son, that all should honor the Son just as they honor the Father.*

> *He who does not honor the Son, does not honor the Father who sent Him.*
>
> *John 5:22, 23 NKJV*

Praying to Get Results!

Prayer is like sports. There's more than one sport, and each game has it's own rules. And the rules are easy to understand!

Believe that the Words of Jesus are true.

> *...your word is truth.*
>
> *John 17:17 NKJV*

You have to believe that there's POWER in the name of Jesus.

You see, the full weight of Heaven is stuffed into that name. Whenever His name is used, it's like bells going off in Heaven. God gives you His full attention, and angels get ready to work, every time they hear you say, *"In the Name of Jesus!"*

> *Jesus came and spoke to them, saying,*
> *All power is given to me in heaven and in earth. Mat. 28:18*
>
> *...Whatever you ask the Father in my name,*
> *He will give it to you. ...ask, and you will receive,*
> *(so) that your joy may be full.*
>
> *John 16,:23, 24*

This is either the truth, or it's a lie!

Heaven's Power is Now on Earth!

After Jesus was tempted in the desert for 40 days and nights, He knew what He was talking about when He said...

> *Repent, for the Kingdom of Heaven is at hand*

At hand means that Heaven is near, it's close, you can see it, hear it, and experience it! The same Power that God uses in Heaven, is now being used on earth:

> This is the power that opens blind eyes, heals the sick, and raises the dead. This power also feeds multitudes of people, and it casts out demons.

Peter knew about this power, that's why he said...

> *my speech and my preaching were ...**in Demonstration***
> *...of the power...*
>
> *1 Cor. 2:4*

Pray, and Ask God for it All

When Peter and John were forbidden to use the *name of Jesus*, they went to their church, and everyone prayed that...

> *...with all boldness they may speak His Word,*
> ***AND*** *that He would stretch out His hand to heal;*
> ***AND*** *that signs and wonders will be done...*
>
> *Acts 4:29, 30*

You see, they wanted to do more than preach. They wanted to be convincing. So they asked God to prove that his words were true (by stretching out His hand to heal, and by performing signs and wonders).

How to Get Specific Instructions

One of the jobs of the Holy Spirit is to give us specific instructions:

> The Holy Spirit gave Ananias specific instructions to go to Saul of Tarsus, and open his blind eyes.   (Acts 9:11-12)

Remember when Jesus gave His disciples specific instructions to untie a colt, and bring it to him. He told them what to say if anyone asked questions (Mat. 21:2, 3). Also, He gave Peter specific instructions on **where to get money** to pay their taxes (Mat. 17:27).

Don't Change Your Mind!

Be willing to believe God's word no matter how long it takes (and it wont be long). This is the kind of mental attitude you need in order to receive good results.

The devil will try to use his **little bit of "doubting power"** to confuse you. This is where the good fight of faith begins. Open your mouth, and tell God what you believe.

Father, I believe what you said in Duet 6:10, that you have given me a beautiful house that I didn't build, filled with all good things; in a large and beautiful city that has everything my family needs.

The Prayer of Binding and Loosing

When you bind someone, they're tied up with ropes or handcuffed. They're restrained, and can't continue their activity. Once they're tied up, they become your prisoners, and can't do anything to hurt you.

When you loose something, you let it go, or release it. That's why you can ask God to **release (or send) angels** to find something you lost, or to fight for you.

In the "spirit world" you're a powerful person, because you belong to a very powerful family—the family of God. In this family, there's the Father, the Holy Spirit, the Lord Jesus, and other sons and daughters. This family is rich and has trillions of angels and Archangels who are assigned to help you. They'll find your lost keys, as well as protect you.

In the "spirit world" you're a powerful person, and you can command satan to **take his hands off** of your money, or your body, and he has to obey and release your property. The devil isn't afraid of you, but he knows who your big brother is, and he's afraid that Jesus will send him to the Lake of Fire before the day of Judgement. (Mat. 8:29)

We have no right to interfere with another person's will (or spirit). In other words, we can't pray and make other people do what we want (except our minor children). **But we do have authority (or control) over demons.**

> *Behold, I give you power ...over all the power of the enemy: and nothing shall by any means hurt you.*
>
> *Luke 10:19*

Jesus gave you control over everything that would hurt you!

We know that no one in their right mind would reject Jesus' offer to save them from Hell. But people have been blinded by unclean spirits. However you've been given power over demons, so you can **bind** the unclean spirits that's blinding your family (or other people).

> *Father, in the Name of Jesus, you said:*
> *...Whatever I bind on earth shall be bound in Heaven,*
> *and whatever I shall loose on earth*
> *shall be LOOSED in heaven.*
>
> *Mat. 18:18*

Now, command satan to let your family members go, in the name of Jesus. And he has to obey your words.

> *Therefore, I bind satan and destroy his control over my son. And in the name of Jesus, satan, I command you to remove the blinders from his eyes. And by faith, Father, I believe that Tommy has received Jesus as his Lord, and he's completely delivered from drugs.*

By faith receive their deliverance and salvation. −You do this by choosing to believe that it's done. Then ask for the right church for each person, because Mat. 12:43 says that unclean spirits come back to their former homes if they're left empty.

The Prayer of Agreement

This prayer requires two or more people who are praying for the same exact thing. It doesn't matter who the people are. They could be all men, all women, couples, or children. Mat. 18:19 says...

> *...if two of you shall agree on earth as touching any thing that **they shall ask, it shall be done for them** of my Father ...*

The Prayer of Faith

Use this prayer when you're praying for **your own desires**. Also, use this prayer if **you** want to do something, or if **you** want to change something.

No one else is included in this prayer. And no one else is praying in agreement with you. Your only requirement is to believe that **you** will receive what you've asked for.

> *...What things soever **you** desire, when ye pray,*
> *believe that **you** receive them, and you shall have them...*
>
> *Mark 11:24*

You have to prove what you believe by doing whatever the Holy Spirit leads you to do.

The Prayer of Praise and Worship

In this prayer, you're not asking God for anything. You're just telling Him how much you love Him. In other words, you're ministering to the Lord (and not to people).

> *...the Father seeketh such to worship Him... John 4:24*

As you can see, God created you to fellowship with Him.

The Prayer of Commitment

This is the prayer you use to cast (or give) all of your problems to God.

> *Casting **all your cares** upon Him; for he cares for you...*
>
> *1 Pet. 5:7*

He wants you to tell Him all of your worries, anxieties, and burdens. **Isn't that what He says to do in Phil. 4:6.**

> *Be anxious for nothing, but in everything by prayer*
> *and* **supplication**,
> *with* **thanksgiving**,
> *let your* **requests** *be made known to God:*

As you can see, if you have a problem, the first step is to cast that problem on the Lord with:

Supplication (Talking, or crying with strong tears, or gut wrenching grief, etc).

In prayer, tell God all of your problems, anxieties, worries, doubts, and fears.
> *Casting all your care upon him; for he careth for you.*
>> *1 Pet. 5:7*

Requests (Asking God for what you want, and believing that His answer is, "Yes!").

Remind Him of His word in Mark 11:24; and ask Him for what you want:

> Put *me in remembrance...*
>> *Isa. 43:26*

Thanksgiving (Giving thanks, and being confident that your request was heard. And believing that you have received it).

And once you ask Him, He wants you to put your complete trust in Him.

> *Commit thy way unto the Lord;*
> *Trust also in him...*
>> *Ps. 37:5*

He is your God who hears and answers prayer. He is your Heavenly Father, and He's going to fix it because He loves you. Just remember to obey his instructions if He requires you to do something.

...and the peace of God, ...will guard your hearts and minds...
Phil. 4:7

Prayer is the Life of a Christian. Without prayer, you couldn't tell God your problems, and He couldn't give you the answers.

The Prayer of Consecration and Dedication

Only once did Jesus pray and end His prayer with *"If it be thy will."* He was hoping that there was a less painful way, one which allowed Him to die more peacefully (without being beat or nailed to a wooden pole). But since God didn't answer Him (or reveal another plan). Jesus said, "Okay, your will be done." In other words, "I already know what your will is, Father, and I'll do it."

Notice that when Jesus raised Lazarus from the dead, He didn't pray, *"If it be thy will."* Because He already knew what the will of God was. Instead, He prayed:

> *Father, I thank You that You have heard Me.*
> *And I know that You always hear Me...*
>
> *John 11:41, 42*

Also when He multiplied the fish and loaves, He simply looked up to Heaven and gave thanks.

Unified Prayer

This prayer is used by **(a prayer group, or an entire congregation)** that is praying together for the same thing. And when each person truly believes that Jesus' words are true, then tremendous power is released from Heaven.

> *And being let go, they (Peter and John) went to their own*
> *company, ...And when they (the prayer group) heard that,*

*they lifted up their voice to God with one accord, and said,
Lord, thou art God, ...And now, Lord, behold their
threatenings, and grant unto thy servants, that with all
boldness **they may speak thy word**. By stretching forth
thine hand to heal; **and that signs and wonders may be
done** by the name of ...Jesus.*

*And when they had prayed, **the place was shaken** where
they were assembled together; and they were all filled with
the Holy Ghost, and they spoke the word of God with boldness...*
Acts. 4:23, 24, 29, 30,
31

Intercessory Prayer

Sometimes you have a burden to get alone and pray. You may not know the person you're praying for, but **you definitely are giving God permission to do something in the earth realm**.

The person you're praying for might live on the other side of the world. But you have to pray until you receive peace in your heart, or until you begin to worship God. This is the indication that the problem has been solved, or that God is involved.

How to Get Your Needs Met

We will briefly talk about each of these simple steps. And when you do them, you'll get good results:

Find the **scriptures** that promise you the things you want (or need).

Ask God for them (in the name of Jesus).

Receive (accept or choose to believe) that God has already created (and made) the things you need. And He will tell you how to get them.

Thank God for it.

Then deal with **the devil**.

Finding the Scriptures

Let's say you want to be healed. Which prayer should you use? Correct!
The "PRAYER OF FAITH" because you want something. Now pray these
scriptures: I Pet. 2:24 and Isa. 53:5.

> Father, your word said that, *(Jesus) bare our sins in his own*
> *body on the tree, that we, being dead to sins, should live*
> *unto righteousness; by whose stripes **you were healed***

You also said:

> *(Jesus) ...was wounded for our transgressions,*
> *he was bruised for our iniquities:*
> *the chastisement of our peace was upon him; and*
> *with his stripes, **we are healed.***

Ask God

Father, your word says:

> *...your Father knows the things you have need of*
>   *before you **ask** Him.*

Mat 6:8

> *...Whatsoever ye shall **ask** the Father*
>   *in my name, he will give it to you...*
>
> ***ask***, *and ye shall receive,*
>   *that your joy may be full.*

John 16:23, 24

How to Receive

You receive by believing that God told you the truth. After that, understand that everything you need was already created. Now, decide if you believe that.

Next, when the Holy Spirit whispers instructions to you, write them down, and make sure you **do them**. Because this is the only way God will give it to you.

This way of living began 2000 years ago when Jesus died on the cross. That's why you have to think, "These things are mine!"

2000 years ago Jesus said, "It is finished!" And if you agree with Him, then say, "My salvation, and my purpose for living, and my wealth has been paid for."

Although these things belong to you now, they were not free. They cost Jesus His life. And He paid that price 2000 years ago. And if you believe this, open your mouth and make some noise, saying, "THIS IS MINE!!!"

So when will you receive these wonderful gifts? ...the moment you believe that God has already created them for you. That's why Mark 11:24 says, *"...receive them, and you shall have them,"* because they belong to you.

> Father, you said in Mark 11:24
> *"...believe it's already mine, and I will have it."*
>
> And in Mat. 7:11, you also said,
> *"Your Father ...gives good things to those who ask Him!"*

Therefore, in the name of Jesus, I choose to believe it belongs to me! And by faith, I take what God said as the truth!

Thank Him!

To thank God, use the prayer of Thanksgiving:

Be anxious for nothing, but in everything by prayer
and supplication,
*with **thanksgiving**,*
let your requests be made known to God:

Phil 4:6 NKJV

"Father, thank you for your word.
Your word says that I'm healed.
And since your word is the truth
I believe that I am healed."

God Always Hears You

God always hears you when you pray.

...this is the confidence that we have in him,
*that, if we **ask any thing***
***according to his will** (which is "His Word")*
he hears us;

God heard your prayer the first time you asked. So there's no need to ask again. But if you feel like you need to pray again, then use the **Prayer of Thanksgiving,** because...

*...if **we know that he hears us**...*
***we know that we have the petitions** that we desired of him.*

1 John 5:14, 15

If you believe that His word is the truth, then confess to God what you believe (regardless) of the pain. Tell Him, "I believe that you heard me. I believe that you told me the truth. And I believe that with Jesus stripes, you've already healed me." Now, keep thanking Him for healing you, even if it takes months before all of the symptoms leave. And don't forget to deal with the devil!

Deal With the devil

God's answer to you is always, Yes! But **He might** require you to do some-thing first. That's why the devil comes–to make sure you don't fulfill the requirement. He'll lie and even kill someone to prevent you from doing what God said. Because he knows that if you disobey God, you wont receive the thing you've asked for.

> So what do we want to do to the devil? That's right. Bind Him! So let's use the prayer of "BINDING AND LOOSING."

When you bind someone, they're tied up with ropes or handcuffs. They can't continue their activity, and they can't hurt you. That's why Jesus told us to pray the Prayer of Binding and Loosing; and God will make sure that satan and his demons are tied up.

> "Father your word says in Mat. 18:18, ...*Whatsoever you **bind** on earth will be bound in heaven*. Therefore, I bind satan and all of his demons and command them to take their hands off of my body, in Jesus' name!"

Why Praying Like This
Will Work

2000 years ago, while nailed to a wooden pole, Jesus said, "It is Finished!" And His work was really finished! Your sins were paid for. Your health was paid for. Your wealth was paid for. Your new home, car, and private school tuition was paid for—in full.

Now all you have to do is ask and receive. (...but don't forget to deal with the devil, because he will come ...*to steal, to kill, and to destroy)*. Then after you've prayed, if the Holy Spirit gives you instructions, then follow them. Because acting on the Word of God is called faith; and faith pleases God, and will always bring good results.

Christmas Everyday

When He ascended on high, He ...gave gifts to men.   Eph. 4:8

Imagine it's Christmas day 2000 years ago, and Jesus places so many gifts under the tree, and they have your name on it. Then He leaves and goes back to Heaven. While there, He's praying for you, and He believes that you will understand that it's God's will for you to open those free gifts. Of course you did unwrap one box. It was the gift of salvation. And there's so many more to open!

Unwrap healing by asking God to heal you based on Isa. 53:5.

> *Jesus was wounded for our transgressions,*
> *He was bruised for our iniquities,*
> *...And by His stripes **we are healed** (because)*
> *God laid on Jesus the iniquity of us all.*
>
> *Isa. 53:5, 6*

Then say, "Father, I believe I am healed." And the Holy Spirit will tell you if you need to do something.

Unwrap the gift of **"doing the kind of work that you love"** by asking God to bless you with wealth and riches and work you love to do.

> *As for every man to whom God has given riches and wealth,*
> *and given him power to eat of it, to receive his portion*
> *and rejoice in his labor–this is the gift of God.*
>
> *Ecc. 5:19 NKJV*

Then say, "Father, I believe I have received from you the work that I love to do." –Then follow the instructions that He gives you.

Now unwrap **the gift of marriage** by looking up the promises, asking for a spouse, and confessing that "you believe that you have already received him (or her) according to Mark 11:24." Then follow any instructions He gives you.

How To Open Your Gifts

Once you believe that these gifts were made available to you 2000 years ago, and that you can accept them right now, then you have to **SAY IT!**

> *...with the heart you believe unto righteousness,*
>   *and with **the mouth** confession is made unto salvation.*
>
> *Rom. 9:10*

Now, take out the words *"righteousness"* and *"salvation"* and replace them with the things you want. For example:

> ...with the heart you believe that you're healed, and with your mouth you confess that you're healed.
> And,
>
> ...with the heart you believe that God supplies your needs, and with your mouth you confess that your needs are provided.

Proof that You Have it

The evidence that you're healed, or that your bills are paid is **"God's Word."** Now you have to believe that. And while you're waiting for it to happen, pray:

> *Father, I thank you that I have received my healing (or my bills paid).*

Don't Ask Again

If you believe that you have received the free gift (or gifts which Jesus paid for with his life) then don't pray for it again, as though God didn't' hear you the first time. This is doubt, because praying again means that you believe that God said, "No, you can't have the free gift!"

If you or others feel the need to pray again, then pray the Prayer of Thanksgiving.

> *Thank you, Father, that you always hear me when I pray.*
> *And I believe I already have it.*
>   (Mark 11:24, 1 John 5:14)

Start Small

Ask yourself, "What can I believe God for?" Then find the scripture, and believe that it's the truth. Ask God for it; then thank Him for it while you're following the Holy Spirit's instructions. And if you're obedient, you will receive it.

The Holy Spirit Wakes People up in the Middle of the Night to Pray for You

> *...the (Holy) Spirit also helps in our weaknesses.*
> *For we do not (always) know (who, or) what we should pray for...*
> *but the Spirit Himself makes **intercession** for us (and others)*
> *with groanings which cannot be uttered.*
>   *Rom. 8:26*

The Holy Spirit wakes people up in the middle of the night to pray for you. Sometimes, they don't know who they're praying for, or what they're praying for, because they're praying in tongues. And **as a result of their obedience to pray, satan's plans against you are cancelled.**

Jesus is Constantly Praying for You

> *...he is able to save ...those who come to God by him,*
> *because he lives forever to make **intercession** for them.*
>   *Heb.7:25 LMSA*

Right now, Jesus is sitting next to God and praying for us (as well as for sinners). After He prays, the Holy Spirit directs Christians to minister to the lost. Then after sinners get saved, the Holy Spirit leads these baby Christians to the information that will help them to stay saved and become successful people.

Don't Curse Your life!

People who habitually continue to sin are those who don't read their Bibles, don't pray, and are always saying what they feel, or what they think—instead of saying what God says.

It's good when you know how to make spiritual laws work for you. But it's another thing to make spiritual laws work against you. For example:

Since you will have what you're always saying;
Choose your words carefully,
and only speak the words that God said.

Stop for a moment and think about what you're saying about your life. What are you saying about your marriage, your spouse, and your children? What are you saying about your job, your business, and your finances?

He who guards his mouth, keeps his life,
but he who opens wide his lips comes to ruin.

Prov. 13:3 AMP

Choose Life

When the enemy attacks you, this is not the time to say something NEGATIVE. **Don't release words that will give the enemy permission to destroy you.** Instead, open your mouth and choose "life" by agreeing with God. Say exactly what God says about you; for example:

"With Jesus wounds, I am healed!" And, *"Because He lives, I will live also. This sickness is not unto death. Therefore, I will not die, but live to proclaim the wonderful acts of God. And the same Spirit that raised Jesus from the dead (also) lives in me, and is giving life to every cell of my body."*

Stop Speaking Negative Words

The devil is a liar, and his words are not true. So the only way to stop speaking lies (negative words) is to replace them with the truth. And God's Word is the truth.

When you're ready to renew your mind, and see results in your life, ask God to direct you to the church where you're suppose to be. That's where you'll learn:

how to **speak** life,
how to **think** right,
how to **imagine** good things for yourself,
how to **receive** the promises of God, and
how to **reject** the devils lies.

When bad things happen, most people think it was *The Will of God*. But in reality, they've broken a spiritual law. They've opened wide their mouths, and made a horrible confession about some area of their lives. For example:

> Sue was furious when Eric came in at 4 a.m. She met him at the door and shouted, "You're nothing but a cheating, lying dog!"

"Well!" You might be saying, "It's the truth!" But how can that be the truth when Jesus said, "I am the way, **the truth** and the life." So if Jesus' words are the truth, then speak the truth about your marriage. For example:

> Hearing his key in the door, Sue was furious when Eric came in at 4 a.m. Sitting up in bed, she prayed, "Father, it is written in your

Word that Eric loves me like Christ loves His church. It is also written that you joined us together, and no one will separate us. And I wont accept anything less. Thank you for showing me what to do in this situation."

When he walked into the bedroom, Sue was confident that God heard her prayer and was guiding her through this situation. Looking in his eyes, she calmly asked her husband, "Eric, where have you been?"

What to Expect When You Pray

...they who seek (or inquire of) the Lord
none of them shall lack any beneficial thing

Psalms 34:10 AMP

Jesus said to ask the Father for what you want, and He wont let you go without your needs met.

...whatsoever you ask for in prayer,
believe that it is granted, ...and you will get it.

Mark 11:24

When you ask God for something, He's going to answer you, and tell you how to get the things you want. And if you want to "receive" them, you'll have to follow His instructions.

...this is the confidence that we have in him,
*...if we **ask any thing according to his will** (which is "His Word")*
he hears us;

You can ask for anything, as long as it's something the Bible says you can have. For instance, it's not God's Will for a man to become pregnant, so if he wants a child, he'll have to ask for his wife to become pregnant.

*And if **we know that he hear us**, whatsoever we ask,*
***we know that we have the petitions** (or things)*
that we desired (or asked) of him.

1 John 5:14-15

You see, God has every intention of giving you what you want. You just have to know how to pray, and believe with confidence that He's already provided it for you.

What Does God Want in Return

The reason you're a Christian today, is because God called you. He called you because He needs you. There's so much work to be done, and He needs your help. So what does He want from you? He wants you to follow His instructions, and **get good results.** This is the way He gets all the glory! And when you tell others about your good results, they'll come to Him too.

You have not chosen me, but I have chosen you
and I have appointed you, ...that you might go and bear fruit...

John 15:16 AMP

You see, God has something specific for you to do. And in order for you to work for Him, He knows that you need peace of mind, so He'll help you.

...so whatever you ask the Father in My Name,
...He may give it to you.

John 15:16

People Who Go Without Their Needs Met

Some Christians read God's instructions, but refuse to do them. For instance, they refuse to forgive others. So when they pray, and don't receive an answer, it's because their sins haven't been forgiven either.

> *...Whenever you stand praying,* **if you have anything against any-**
> **one,** *forgive him and let it drop, ...in order that your Father who is*
> *in heaven may also forgive you your [own] failings and shortcom-*
> *ings...*
>
> *But* **if you do not forgive,**
> *neither will your Father in heaven forgive*
> *your [failings] and shortcomings.*
>
> *Mark 11:25, 26 AMP*

Another reason people go without their needs met is because of disobedience. They don't follow God's instructions in order to get the things that
they want. In this case, it's not God's fault.

Another reason is not **saying** what they believe. And the reason they don't
say certain things, is because they don't believe that they'll get it. Here's
my version of what Jesus said in Mark 11:23.

> *"Whatever I believe that God will do for me, I have to say it,*
> *and I'll get it."*

Also, there are times when God tells you **not** to read a certain book. You
might think that the book will help you, but He knows that once you believe
something, then it's hard for you to believe Him when He tells you something different. For instance, if the book says that people with your symptoms will die, it'll be hard to believe God when He says, "You're going to
live."

The Right Way to Pray

> *...put the Lord in remembrance [of His promises],*
> *keep not silence*
>
> *Isa. 62:6 AMP*

There are times, when God will promise you something directly through
your spirit. And if you have any doubts, you can ask Him to give you **scriptures to support** what He said.

After you find the scriptures, pray (asking for those promises). The Holy Spirit will speak to you, and you must listen carefully. When He's finish speaking, ask Him questions if you need to. Write down His instructions, and make them a priority.

If you forget what He told you, repent, and you'll be forgiven. Ask again, and the instructions will be repeated.

Throughout the day, when the enemy talks to you, open your mouth, and remind God of the promises He made to you. This will cause your joy to return, and depression will leave.

God wants you to remind Him of what He said, because **when you get what you've asked for**, then you'll know that His Words are true. And each time your prayers are answered, your confidence in Him will grow.

The Wrong Way to Pray

God will not use His power to change our circumstances just because we beg, plead, cry, shout, or run around the church. He's not moved by burning candles, or having convulsions.

You can love God with all of your heart, and talk about how sweet He is all day long, but God still wont move. But **Jesus told us how to get God to change our circumstances...**

> *The person who has My commands (or my Words)*
> *and keeps them (or obeys them)*
> *is the one who (really) loves Me (Jesus)*
>
> *and whoever (really) loves Me (and obeys my Words),*
> *will be loved by My Father*
>
> *John 14:21*
>
> *...And we will come to him and make Our home with him.*
>
> *(vs. 23)*

Since God only responds to His own Words, we're required to do some light work, which is to search the scriptures. Because the Bible is the major way God speaks to us. And whatever we don't understand, the Holy Spirit will explain it, or **He'll direct us** to a good teacher, a book, or a CD.

Some Christians don't search for scriptures. They want to depend on **dreams, visions, angels, and prophesies**. The problem with this is that if a green angel appeared, and instructed them to fly to Africa and start a church, they wouldn't know if this was from God or not.

Mark 11: 24 says to, *"..Ask in prayer."*

It doesn't say to, *"...think, ...or hope, ...or wish."*
Instead it says to, "...**Ask**." So don't keep silent.

Remember, the only thing an "unspoken prayer request" produces, is an "unspoken answer" from God.

Ask God What to Do

If you don't know what to do, look at what the word of God says in James 1:5...

If any of you lack wisdom
let him ask of God
that giveth to all men liberally
and upbraideth not
and it shall be given him

In other words, "If you have a question, God wants you to ask Him. He will answer all of your questions without finding fault. He promises to answer you.

God wants you to come to Him first, and He wants you to expect to get the answer. Although it'll be an answer you can live with, it might offend other people. Why? Because your actions might be different from what they've been taught.

> *But let him ask in faith, nothing wavering*
> *For he that wavereth is like a wave of the sea*
> *driven with the wind and tossed. ...let not that man think*
> *that he shall receive any thing of the Lord.*
>
> *James 1:6-7*

You'll remain in your situation, if you don't do what God told you to do.

How to Know When You're Obeying God

When God tells you to do something, you'll have peace when you obey Him. He didn't say that you wouldn't have doubts about how things will turn out, or that you wouldn't be scared.

Your job is to trust Him, and do what He said, even if you're afraid, or tired. Because... Christians who get good results are those who follow God's instructions, even though it doesn't make sense. They understand that doing things their own way (without consulting) God is not wise.

How to Know When You're Not Obeying God

When the Holy Spirit reminds you of what God said, you find yourself switching to a different thought. And you continue doing things that you know wont work. And every time you do it, you have a feeling of condemnation.

Condemnation is a feeling that something is wrong. It's a feeling like getting into the bathtub with your clothes on, or like walking up a hill with a very heavy load.

FAITH TO STAY MARRIED

The Difference Between Faith and Belief

Belief is what you believe. It's what you think is true. But Faith is "doing" what you believe. In other words, if it's true, you should be doing it.

You can believe a lot of things, but until you actually "do" what you believe, nothing will happen.

> You can believe that one day you're going to get a new car. But you wont get a new car until you do something to get the car. You have to **use your faith.** And in this case, using your faith means to work, save some money, and then buy the car.

Do the Word

If we believe that God's word is the truth, then we should do it. For instance:

With worry, we should do Phil. 4:6.

With fear, we should do II Tim. 1:7.

With our bills, we should do Mark 11:24 and pray Phil 4:19.

With confusion we should do James 1:5.

Common Sense vs. Faith

God's instructions to you may not make any kind of logical sense whatsoever! For instance, He might tell you to do something that you've never done before. And although you might be shy, you have to do it in order to get the benefits.

Joshua received strange instructions, but he obeyed, and received good results.

> "...walk around the city one time (for seven days) without talking. And on the seventh day, walk around the city seven times; then shout, and the wall will fall down."

But couldn't God have done it another way? Why didn't He just send a tornado and blow the wall down. Then the Israelites could have rushed in and taken the city much sooner.

Although one might think they were exhausted after walking seven times around the city, the point is that they took the city, and they did it God's way, and were successful.

When it Doesn't Make Sense

Disappointment comes when people ask God for something, and it doesn't happen. The reason it doesn't happen, is because when they hear His voice, they refuse to obey (because His instructions don't make sense to them).

But obeying God has nothing to do with making sense:

> **It didn't make sense** when Jesus told the lepers
> to go show themselves to the priest?

> **And it didn't make sense** when Jesus told Peter to get
> out of the boat and walk on water.

But when they obeyed, they got good results!

The Difference between Faith and Common Sense

There is a difference between faith and common sense. Common sense, is wearing your left shoe on your left foot. But faith is doing what God tells you to do—even if it doesn't make sense.

> *Jesus said to the lepers "**Go**, show yourself to the priest."*
> *And as **they went**, they were cleansed.*

Notice how power was released (from God) to heal the lepers, as soon as they started doing what Jesus told them to do. And...

> Imagine the power God will release to help you,
> when you obey the voice of His Holy Spirit.

God said, *The just shall live by faith...* not by common sense. But since we have (a little) wisdom of our own, we think we know what's best. However, when we **obey the voice of the Holy Spirit**, we're actually following God's instructions; and each time we do, we get good results. When we get good results, we know it wasn't by our own wisdom–**so we have to give God all of the Credit!**

Being Humbled Comes Before Honor

> *...before honor is humility.*
>
> *Prov. 15:33 NKJV*

I'm sure Joshua and the Israelites felt humiliated when they walked around the wall of Jericho. And the smelly lepers felt humiliated when they had to walk down the street. And Jesus felt humiliated nailed to a wooden pole while people were laughing at Him.

So why would God allow us to be humiliated before giving us a great blessing.

And you shall remember that the Lord your God led you all the way these forty years in the wilderness, to humble you and test you, to know what was in your heart, whether you would keep His commandments or not.

So He humbled you, allowed you to hunger ...that He might make you know that man shall not live by bread alone; but man lives by every word that proceeds from the mouth of the Lord.

Duet. 8:2, 3 NKJV

God turns us into the people He wants us to be. He protects us and takes care of us until we learn to walk by faith, and not by sight.

What it Means to be Humbled

In order to receive great blessings from God, we have to do things His way. We have to be willing to be ridiculed, talked about, lied on, maybe even humiliated. **This is the attitude Abraham had when he was about to offer Isaac in obedience to God**.

Just think about something that God told you to do in the past, but you didn't do it because satan said, "If you do that, people are going to laugh at you."

Maybe you didn't do it because your friends or your spouse wasn't in agreement with you. But later, when you missed out on your blessing, you learned that the next time you're inspired to do something, you don't need anyone else's approval.

We Want to Do it Our Way

Naaman was given instructions to wash 7 times in the Jordan river. But instead of washing, he went away angry. He was hoping that the prophet Elisha would come out and wave a magic wand over him, or at least tell him to wash in a cleaner river. (2 Ki. 5:8-12)

You see, this man's problem was his pride. He thought he was to important to obey the prophet's insignificant instructions. But when he stopped thinking of his own reputation, and began to obey God, he was healed.

God Wants All of the Credit!

When you get the final results, and you're shouting for joy, one thing is for sure, "God did it!" And this is the way He gets the credit.

So you see, God may not lead you to go to the best hospital, or give you the Pastor for your husband, or lead you to apply for a loan. Instead, He might give you instructions that doesn't make sense to you.

Stop Wasting Time

Time is like money. Spend it wisely. Just go ahead and obey God, and get the results you want.

His instructions might seem like a waste of time, but by the time you try to do things your own way, then 5, 10, 15 or 20 years might have gone by (with no results). And there's no point in praying to die so you can go to Heaven. Just start obeying Him.

Now here's a good example of saving time:

> During the wedding at Cana of Galilee, they ran out of wine.
> So Jesus told the servants what to do, ...and they did it ...and the water was made wine. (John 2:7-9)

But notice, the water would not have been made wine unless the servants obeyed Jesus. They had to **risk the humiliation of being fired** for bringing water, instead of wine. But they believed Jesus, so they acted on His words and received good results.

When is the Miracle Going to Happen?

If you obey what God is telling you to do, while you're on your way, the miracle will happen. Your faith activates the power of God. In other words, it's activated after you **act** like the word of God is true.

Faith Works by Love

Did you ever wonder why the servants obeyed Jesus, and filled six giant jars with water? They did it because they believed in Him; and obeying Him was more important than anything else. Did they take a risk? Well, Jesus said "Wise men hear His words and do them, but foolish men hear, and disobey." So the real risk is not doing what He says.

Friendship With the World
Makes You
an Enemy of God

"Not really!" you might be shouting in your defense. But you have to decide if you want people to **think you're normal** by telling them that you're broke, or sick.

Yes, your friends might **think you're normal** if you can't pay your bills, and if you're always sick. And you might get their pity and sympathy, but nothing will change unless you do things God's way.

You see, the Holy Spirit is leading, pushing, and pulling on some Christians to get remarried. But they're like mules, heavily burdened with the wrong thinking, and they wont move.

Great Faith

"Forget my friends and family! Just say it Lord, and I'll do it!"

Great faith is asking God for something and being sure that He'll get it for you.

Great faith is telling people that you believe that you already have it.

And great faith is doing whatever you're led to do to get it (even if it doesn't make sense).

Great faith is not only what you believe, but also what you do.

Faith is following instructions without doubting, or trying to figure it out, and without asking questions.

Faith is obeying regardless of your tradition, the weather, or any other circumstance.

I say to one soldier "Go," and he goes;
and to another, "Come," and he comes;
*and to another, "Do this," and **he does it**.*

Mat. 8:9

The centurion asked Jesus to "say one word" because he was prepared to obey Him. He understood the importance of obedience because his soldiers always obeyed him. When he had finished speaking, Jesus said that he had great faith..

Have Faith in God

...when you pray ...believe you receive them,
and you shall have them.

Mark 11:24

The God-Kind of Faith

God uses His faith to make things. He thinks about what He wants, and then He says, *"Let there be!..."* And that's what He gets.

You use the God-Kind of faith every time you talk about something you believe. You also use the God-Kind of faith whenever you make a prediction about what's going to happen with the weather, your circumstances, your job, your marriage, or your finances.

The God-Kind of faith is believing **that whatever you say with your mouth is going to happen.**

In the Kingdom of God, you have to speak words with your mouth before anything will happen.

Your words are an indication of what you believe. For instance, if you hear yourself say, "...God supplies all of my needs" then this is what you will believe. But if you hear yourself say, "I don't have any money" you will believe that instead.

How to Get the God-Kind of Faith

faith comes by hearing ...the word of God.

Rom. 10:17

When you **hear** the Bible being taught, suddenly you believe that you can do anything! ...But you can't stop there, because you're only **believing**.

What God does, is He **SAYS** what He believes; and after that, it actually happens.

Jesus said:

> *...I have given them **the words** which you gave me;*
> *and they have received them.*

John 17:8

God gave us His word, so we would speak His **exact words.** And those words will change our lives.

When we're sick, we take medicine because we believe that it will make us well. We continue to cough, to sneeze, and to blow our nose while taking the medicine because we believe that if we keep taking it, we'll eventually be well.

The reason we have so much confidence in the medicine, is because someone told us that the medicine would heal us. Well, someone also told us that, *"...with Jesus stripes, we have already been healed."*

Who's Right in the Sight of God

> *...the righteousness of God ...comes by believing ...and*
> *...reliance on Jesus*
>
> *Rom. 3:22 Amp*

God says that you're "right" **when you believe** that Jesus told you the truth (about getting saved, or being healed, or making more money, etc...).

God also calls you *"righteous"* **when you prove** that you believe His word (by following the instructions you receive from the Holy Spirit).

The Name of Jesus

The key to activate the power of God is *"The Name of Jesus."*

> *...Whatsoever you ask the Father in my name,*
> *He will give it to you... ask, and you will receive,*
> *(so) that your joy may be full.*
>
> *John 16:23, 24*

Jesus told you to use His name because in Heaven, the Father honors *the name*; and on earth, demons stop and obey *that name.*

*Therefore **God has highly exalted him, (Jesus)***
***and given him a name** which is above every name:*
*That **at the name of Jesus** every knee should bow,*
*of **things in heaven** (angels bow before him),*
*and **things in earth** (sickness, poverty, and divorce bow before*
Him);
*and **things under the earth** (the devil, his demons, and*
hell also bow);

Phil. 2:9-10

God awarded Jesus with this power after He fearlessly faced punishment and death for all men.

No other name is given that will save men from hell, or heal their bodies, or prosper them financially. The *Name of Jesus* is superior to all other names. It's greater than the name of cancer, and AIDS, and divorce, and even death!

satan is No Match for Jesus

"The Name of Jesus" will always **stop satan**. Whatever he's doing, he'll stop and become paralyzed with fear because he knows that someone greater than himself has shown up. He's no match for Jesus. All power in Heaven, and on earth has been given to Jesus, and **no spirit dare defy the laws of God.**

satan knows that if you use the *"Name of Jesus"* the power of God will show up. And if you command him to stop in the *Name of Jesus*, he has to stop, because **God created laws that both (men and spirits) must obey**.

You Are Not Powerless

Jesus said: *...**I have given you authority ...to overcome all the power of the enemy;** nothing will harm you.*

Luke 10:19 NIV

We are not Powerless!! Jesus is God, and He gave us power to **change our circumstances**, and power to **recover what was stolen**. Power to restore our health, and power to excel regardless of our disadvantages. He gave us Power to continue, when others are quitting. And power to prosper, regardless of the economy.

The reason the devil can't touch you is because God raised you up with Christ, and MADE you sit with Christ (on the right hand of God) far above demons, devils, and wicked spirits. Psalms 91 says, *"We live (safely) under the shadow of the almighty."* And no demon is courageous enough to come under God's enormous shadow—where we live.

The Power is Already in You

> *...him that is able to do exceeding, abundantly,*
> *above all that we ASK or THINK,*
> *according to **the power that worketh in us***
>
> > *Eph. 3:20*

The "Power of God" is His Word. And when you believe that His Word is the truth, the word becomes alive in your heart, and God begins to work inside of you, outside of you, and all around you. He begins working throughout your community, throughout the world, and even throughout the universe; to do exceedingly, abundantly, above all that you could ask or think.

> *...I am not ashamed of **the gospel of Christ:***
> *For **it is the power of God**...*
>
> > *Rom. 1:16 NKJV*

You see, the power of God is in you. And God will make His power work for you depending upon **the scriptures you (believe are true).** So if you want God to do more for you, begin to study His promises. And when you believe that God can do more, He will!

God can't lie, or deceive you. His Word can't return to Him void, it must accomplish what it was sent to do (as long as you follow His directions).

> *...What things soever ye **desire**, ...ye shall have them.*
>
> *Mark 11:24*

Do you want something **so bad** that you're willing to obey God to get it? (Because that's the only way He'll give it to you).

Everything Works by Laws

Spiritual laws allow us to complete our God-given assignments in the short-est amount of time. And natural laws, like traffic laws, help us to reach our destinations without premature deaths, injuries, and delays.

The Law of Faith

> *Where is boasting then? It is excluded.*
> *By what law? Of works?*
> *No, but by **the law of faith**.*
>
> *Rom. 3:27 NKJV*

Whatever you received on this earth, you got it by *"The law of faith."*

You don't need *"faith"* for the things you can see, touch, taste, smell, and hear.

Faith is needed for the things you can't see, and for the things you don't have. For instance, if you want a fur coat, God requires that you **believe that He's going to give it to you.**

> *...And you shall have it*
>
> *(Mark 11:24)*

Of course, in order to receive anything from God, you'll have to follow His instructions.

What Are Miracles

Everything God does is a miracle. **It's a miracle that we can hear the Holy Spirit, and obey His voice, and get good results.**

It's a miracle that God gave us His Words, so we could speak them. And when God hears a man's voice and answers Him, that's also a miracle!

The Way You Work for God

Look at all the miracles God did through Moses. Notice that God was telling Moses what to say, and what to do. And when Moses obeyed, God performed the miracles. This is how it was with Jesus, and this is how it works with us.

Your Words Give Life

Jesus said, the Words that I speak to you are Spirit and they are Life.

When Jesus spoke, His words weren't for flesh to hear. His words were for Spirits to hear. He would talk to God, satan, or to a person's spirit. For instance, **when a little girl died**, Jesus told her spirit to return to her body.

Your Words Can Kill

When Jesus spoke to **the fig tree**, the purpose of His words was to remove the life from that tree. He was not talking to the wood. He was talking to the life that was in the tree. Therefore, when He spoke, God heard Him, and sent an angel to destroy that tree.

In the same way, Christians have to live according to *the law of faith.* In other words, the words that we speak, determine what we get out of life.

Faith Means Work

When God speaks, He expects to have what He says. And since He made our spirits in *His image* and in *His likeness,* when we speak, we should expect to have what we say. Why? Because we're like God. *We rule (in this life) as Kings (Rev. 5:10).* **What happens when kings speak? They have what they say**!

You can ask for anything, and God will tell you where to **go,** what to **say,** and what to **do**–to get the things you need, or desire. This is the way things are done in the Kingdom of God.

When you obey His voice, He's faithful to give you what you want. He'll even drive out unthankful people from fabulous neighborhoods, and give you their houses, their jobs, and their businesses (Duet. 6:10-11).

How the devil Steals

When we try to keep our marriages together, or improve our health, or operate a business (without hearing from God) it's like building a house with our eyes closed.

You see, the devil steals from those who rely upon their own wisdom. The devil knows that when he attacks their family, their health, or their money, most Christians will rebuke him—and stop at that.

Although Jesus said to cast out demons, as soon as the demons are cast out, many Christians will call someone on the phone and start talking about what the devil did, and how unfortunate they are. This kind of **speaking** will only allow satan to return and continue stealing.

While you're waiting for God to give you the strategy on how to deal with a problem, He wants you to confess (or admit) that your life is exactly what He said it is:

> *"...I'm blessed in the city and blessed in the country. I'm*
> *blessed coming in, and blessed going out.*
> *...and whatever I do with my hands prospers. ...my God*
> *supplies all of my needs. ...And I'm already healed!*

Also, when you mention " *...many are the afflictions of the righteous"* always include *"...but God delivers me out of them all."*

When satan asks, *"Will God deliver you this time?"* Your reply should be, *"Yes, because...*

> *...It has been written, Man shall not live by bread alone,*
> *but by **every word** that comes from the mouth of God."*

Mat. 4:4

God can hear and talk. So when you ask Him a question, expect an answer. If His answer contains instructions, **this is the battle plan** that will lead you to take possession of the things you want.

> *So shall my word be that goeth forth out of my mouth:*
> *It shall not return unto me void (without producing),*
> *but **it shall accomplish** that which I please,*
> *and **it shall prosper** in the thing whereto I sent it.*

sa. 55:11

You know the Word. But now it's time to start practicing it! Why? So the devil wont steal anything else from you.

How Not to Get Blessed

The way not to get blessed is by doing what Eve did. —She heard God, but she ignored His instructions.

Peter would have missed his blessing too, if he had said, "I fished all day, but I didn't catch anything. **No!** Jesus, I'm not going back out there."

The foul-smelling lepers could have said, "**No!** We could get killed showing ourselves to the Priest. We're not healed, but at least we're alive!"

And the servants at the wedding feast could have said, "**No!** Are you trying to get us fired? Man, if we brought water to the Governor, we could loose our jobs!"

Created In His Image

And God said let us make man... in our image, after our likeness...
Gen. 1:26

How could we be like God? He's sinless, He can't die, and He knows everything! Well, God already knew that without His help, we couldn't be like Him. That's why He said, "Let US make man!"

You see, **Jesus** volunteered to die for our sins. And now that we're sinless, we can live forever just like God. And the **Holy Spirit** agreed to tell us everything necessary to live successfully. Wow! With their help, we are like God.

Understanding is Extremely Important!

There are two ways to understand something. You can understand natural (intellectual) things. And you can understand spiritual things which are revealed to your spirit (but not to your mind). Once you understand something, you'll think, speak, and act like it's true.

You have two sets of eyes. **Your physical body have eyes, and your spiritual body have eyes**. You also have natural ears and spiritual ears. Jesus said, "He who have ears to hear, let him hear."

When you understand spiritual things, it means that **the eyes of your spirit are opened**. And when your spiritual eyes are open, you begin to see the possibilities that you couldn't see before. You become convinced that God said, "Yes! you can have it."

You Have Three Parts

You are **a spirit**. And your spirit is made in the image and likeness of God (it will live forever).

You have **a soul**, which is your (mind, will, and emotions).

Lastly, your spirit lives in **a body**. Your body is the vehicle which gets you around on the earth.

Once you're born again, you're not suppose to act on your own. The Holy Spirit tells you exactly where God wants you to go, and what to do when you get there. There is no reason to fail, because the Holy Spirit is always with you.

> *Then God said, "Let Us make man in Our image,*
> *according to Our likeness; let them have dominion (which is*
> *territory to rule over)*

Gen. 1:26

Our spirits are made in God's image, and we rule just like Him with our words. How? Simple. Whatever we say is created for us by the angels (Ps. 103:20).

Meet God

> *In the beginning was the Word... and the Word was God.*

John 1:1

Well, **if the Word (was) God—then the Word (is still) God**. Everything we know about God, we got from His word. **If the Bible was completely taken out of us, we would not know God.**

The Spirit World

There is a spirit world where God, Jesus, and the Holy Spirit lives. And the holy angels live there too. But so does satan and his demons, who lie, steal, and kill. Therefore, the only way to protect ourselves is by obeying God's word.

Although we live in a body, our spirits also participate in the activity of the spirit world. We pray to God, we're led by the Holy Spirit, we see visions, we have dreams, and we use our imaginations.

Christians are well known in the spirit world as God's children. And satan is afraid of them. The biggest weapon he uses against them is lying. He lies to them if they don't know who they really are, and if they don't know what belongs to them as sons and daughters of a King.

Christians who get good results are those who follow God's instructions, even though it doesn't make sense. They understand that doing things their own way (without consulting God) is not wise.

Tired of Doing Things
the World's Way?

The Holy Spirit will guide you out of the world's system and change the way you do business. He is your teacher, your guide, and your helper.

Whether your assignment is to raise children, operate an organization, or to preach the gospel, you will be given "Power" to be successful.

Money is your servant. Use it to do what God tells you to do with it. His Holy Spirit tells you where to get the money you need. He might tell you to hold a seminar, write a book, or return to school. He might miraculously cancel your debt, or you might receive unexpected checks in the mail, or people might give you money, etc...

God has a thousand ways to get money to you. So be sure not to use your age, weight, nationality, financial status, education, neighborhood, marital status, or health, to limit God.

> *But ye shall receive power, after that the Holy Ghost is come upon you: and ye shall be witnesses unto me both in Jerusalem, and in all Judea, and in Samaria, and unto the uttermost part of the earth.*
>
> *Acts 1:8*

The Holy Spirit is in you now, but when He is ready to work, He doesn't stay in your belly. Like smoke, He rises up and covers your body, empowering you to do the impossible.

Don't risk losing your anointing by displeasing God or "Grieving His Holy Spirit." He gave you His tender, sweet, compassionate, and loving Holy Spirit. Please do not grieve Him. **He's all we've got.**

God loves you and He will demonstrate His love for you with action, not only with words or feelings. (1 Cor. 2:4)

Beloved, it's not God who keeps people poor, unmarried, unhappy, or sick and tired. It's what they have been taught to expect from God. The reason people want to die and go to heaven is because they've been taught that when they get there, they will be rewarded.

With some people, there's no doubt about it (and no questions asked) when they get to Heaven, they will receive unlimited wealth, and excellent health. –But why not teach the body of Christ to expect the same treatment on Earth, (as it is in Heaven).

> *...thy will be done on Earth,* ***as it is in Heaven****!*

You see, on earth, money is needed to promote the gospel; and excellent health is needed to complete our assignments–we must receive both!

God Loves You

He that spared not his own Son, ...will also ...freely give us all things?

Rom. 8:32

How has God loved you? The Bible says that He sent Jesus to remove your sins, your poverty, and your diseases? Mark 11:22-24 tells us that all God wants from us is to BELIEVE HIM.

If things haven't worked out in the past ten, twenty, or thirty years, don't you think it's time to start listening to the Holy Spirit rather than to people?

People may give you scriptures on how you should live your life, but those may not be the scriptures God wants to give you.

God Needs Your Body

*I beseech (or make a request of) you, ...by the mercies of God, that you present (give) **your bodies** a living sacrifice (which is a vessel of obedience)...*

Rom. 12:1

This scripture doesn't say, "give God your spirit." It says, give Him your body. The way to give your body as a living sacrifice, is by **making yourself available for the work He wants to do through you.** Your body is a container for Him and His word. Therefore, decide to be a vessel of honor, filled with God and His word (which is His power).

But in a great house there are not only vessels of gold and of silver, but also of wood and of earth; some for formal use on occasions of honor and others for service.

If therefore a man purifies himself from these things, he will become like a vessel pure for honor, worthy of the master's use, and ready for every good work.

II Tim. 2:20-21 LMSA

To be a vessel of honor, you have to let God use you anyway He desires. Flesh and blood can offer guidance and counsel, but only the Spirit of God can give true direction and meaning to your life.

I Therefore, the prisoner of the Lord, beseech (request of) you that you walk worthy of the vocation (or job) in which you are called (or assigned),

Eph. 4:1

Walk as He would have you to walk—to please Him, not people. He saved you, and only He can preserve your life. Make it your business to find out what God wants to do with your life. This includes your job, your church, and the ministry you're called to do.

God Works, Too!

Jesus said, the Father in me does the work.

Does God ...WORK MIRACLES
*...because **you believe what you heard?** Gal. 3:5 NIV*

God works everyday, and all night long. We call His work "Miracles." And the reason He works miracles among you is because **you believe** what He told you in the Bible (or you believe what you've heard in your spirit). And the way He knows that you believe, is because you actually obey.

The Holy Spirit

While reading this scripture, don't stop here...

No eye has seen, no ear has heard, no mind has conceived what God has prepared for those who love him...

Keep reading...

> **BUT God has revealed it to us by his (Holy) Spirit.**
> *...even the deep things of God ...(so) that we may understand what God has freely given (to) us.*
>
> *1 Cor. 2:10-12*

God gave us His (Holy) Spirit because He wants us to know His thoughts, which includes His plans and purpose for our lives.

> *The (Holy) Spirit searches ALL THINGS,*
> *even THE DEEP THINGS of God.*

Without the Holy Spirit, people couldn't hear (or understand) God's plans.

The Wisdom of God

God's wisdom existed before the earth was made..

> *I (wisdom) was established ...from the beginning,*
> *before God created the earth.*
>
> *Prov. 8:23*

God's wisdom is His thoughts and ideas. When He gives us His "wisdom," He is telling us what's on His mind.

Before He created the mountains, they were first an idea in His mind. He could see them in His imagination; and then He spoke, "Let there be...!"

In His wisdom, God decided where the oceans would be.

> *When he gave to the sea its bounds,*
> *that the waters should not transgress his commandment...*
> **I together with him was establishing them**
>
> *Prov. 8:29-30 LMSA*

The Purpose of the Anointing

..in that day (satan's) burden will be lifted from your shoulders, (and his) yoke from your neck; (satan's) yoke will be broken **because of (God's) anointing.**

Isa. 10:27

What is the anointing? **The anointing is the Powerful Spirit of God that is in you.**

...you shall receive POWER
when **the Holy Spirit has come upon you**

Acts 1:8

The anointing is God speaking and working through you. And people think that it's you doing the miracles, but it's really God.

And **the Spirit of the Lord will come upon you**, *and you*
...will be turned into another man.

1 Sam. 10:6

At twelve, Jesus enjoyed reading the WORD. He understood the Old Testament, and could easily explain the scriptures. And all of this took place before the Holy Spirit descended upon Him.

...when He was twelve years old, ...they found Him in the temple sitting in the midst of the teachers, both listening to them and asking them questions. And all who heard Him were astonished at His UNDERSTANDING and ANSWERS. ...And Jesus increased in WISDOM...

Luke 2:42, 46, 48, 52

Although Jesus studied God's Word and TALKED to the elders, **He didn't have the POWER to heal** anyone until He was filled with the Holy Spirit.

The Holy Spirit is God. And God has POWER:

...God anointed Jesus
...with the Holy Spirit and with POWER...
*...for **God was with Him***

Acts 10:38

Do you see the part that says, *"...for God was with Him."* This means that
God was living inside of Jesus, and He was doing the miracles.

*...**God was in Christ**, reconciling the world to himself...*

2 Cor. 5:19

So when you're anointed, it means that you're filled with the Holy Spirit
(who is God), and He's working through you to speak and perform miracles.

When he had been baptized, ...the heavens were opened to Him,
*...He saw **the Spirit of God** descending ...upon Him.*

...you shall receive POWER
when the Holy Spirit has come upon you

Acts 1:8

After Jesus was anointed with the Holy Spirit, He was able to hear God's
voice, receive instructions, heal people, feed multitudes, walk on water, and
RISE from the dead.

*And **suddenly a voice** came from heaven,*
*...Then **Jesus was led** by the Spirit ...*

Mat. 3:16, 17;   Mat. 4:1

The Kingdom of God is Within You

God lives in you. He rules on Earth, through you. And the reason He gets
great pleasure when you profit, is because He gets all the glory (or credit).

The reason God wants you to be in control, is because when you're the Boss, (or
the person in charge) He can do so many good things for people, through you.

When you obey the Holy Spirit, you 're proving to God that you trust Him.

Here's my version of Heb. 11:6.

> *He who comes to God must believe that He (is real)*
> *and that He rewards those who*
> *diligently (make every effort to find) Him.*

Q.   Does Jesus perform miracles? Or God?

A.   *Jesus said, "...The Father **in me** does the work.*

Jesus knew that God was inside of Him, and was causing miracles to happen on the earth. Even His mother knew it, that's why she said...

> *"...Whatsoever he (Jesus) saith unto you, **DO IT!** "*
>
> John 2:5

In order to get your needs met, God has to work for you. But in order for Him to work for you, He needs you to do your part first. And that's simply to believe, and obey!

Q.   What pleases God?

A.   Faith. God is looking for a relationship with Christians who are committed, and faithful. They study and practice living by His words. They have a strong desire to please Him, and they follow His instructions. As a result, God is always working through them. (John 15:4-10).

CHOOSING TO REMAIN SINGLE

Q. After my divorce, I decided to live alone for the rest of my life. Is this my choice to make?

A. You can decide to live alone for the rest of your life, but if you have any regrets, you can always change your mind, and ask God for His perfect will for your life.

> *For the Kingdom of God is ..righteousness,*
> *peace, and joy, in the Holy spirit.*
>
> *Rom. 14:17*

Righteousness means to do things God's way. And His desire is for you to have peace and joy. He doesn't want you to jump up and down shouting in church, and then go home lonely, depressed, and unhappy. Instead He wants you to rejoice, because...

> *... it is your Father's good pleasure to give you*
> *(all of the good things that) the Kingdom (provides).*
>
> *Luke 12:32*

This means that God gets pleasure when you have peace and joy as a result of obeying His instructions.

Q. If a church forbids divorce and remarriage, can a person live a normal life alone?

A. I Tim. 4:1-3 clearly teaches that forbidding to marry is wrong.

Without the gift of celibacy, few can live single without committing fornication. When people are forced to suppress their sexual desires, they become angry by such oppressive rules, and they will secretly satisfy their sexual needs.

People are forced to pretend that they're obeying the rules, especially those who have positions in the church. As a result, some of them will die prematurely from sexually transmitted diseases, and never experience the joy of completing their God-given assignments.

Q. **When the church forbids divorced people to get remarried, do they become eunuchs?**

A. No, because a eunuch is a castrated male whose penis was cut off as a result of violence, war, or a tragic accident. Also, we've all read about the few African cultures that practice castrating young girls. They believe that this would prevent them from having sex before marriage. But this type of mutilation makes it difficult for them to later become wives and mothers.

> *...others were made that way by men;*
>
> *Mat. 19:12*

The Bible refers to eunuchs who have positions of great authority, such as attendants over the king's harem, or being in charge of the queen's gold.

> *...a man of Ethiopia, a eunuch of great authority under Candace, the Queen of the Ethiopians, who had charge of all her treasury, and had come to Jerusalem to worship,*
>
> *Acts 8:27*

Some people are born with mental or physical handicaps, and they're incapable of having sex.

> *For some are eunuchs because they were born that way;*
>
> *Mat. 19:12*

Some widows, divorcees, and virgins, have decided to work full-time for the Lord without the distractions of having a family. However, this isn't the *"natural gift of celibacy."* It's a decision that the person makes, and therefore sexual desires will come.

and others have renounced marriage because of the kingdom of heaven.
Mat. 19:12

That's why the Apostle Paul said:

> *...I counsel younger widows to marry,*
> *to have children, and to manage their homes...*
1 Timothy 5:14 NIV

After a divorce or the death of a spouse, there isn't anyone to have sex with, so people become celibate, not eunuches.

Your Sexuality

Just as sexuality is viewed differently in each household, sexuality is viewed differently in each denomination. This is one of the main reasons why this book was written. Because although Christians have different views regarding sex, one thing we can all do, and that is to read the Word of God.

Christians come from a varied background of sexual experiences before coming to Christ, and some people think that everyone had the same experiences that they had; but most people haven't!

Please understand that people do experience changes in their sexuality after being abused or raped. And some will hate **the idea** of making love to the opposite sex, and others will feel a strong need to please abusive men (or women). But like everyone else, victims of rape and sexual abuse need to be born-again and filled with the Holy Spirit; and God will help them.

There are people who were born with two sets of genitals. And to often, those born with two genitals have the wrong one removed at birth. Instead of waiting for the child to reach sexual maturity, the doctors allow the parents to choose the baby's gender, only to find out later that they've made a terrible mistake.

In all of the above-cases, the Holy Spirit will direct these Christians to their mates (if they have a desire to get married).

Unfortunately, there are people in the church who are confused about their sexuality, and as a result of not understanding the scriptures, they teach people to think like they do.

Q. What are the advantages to remaining single?

A. *There is a difference also between a wife and a virgin. The unmarried woman careth for the things of the Lord, that she may be holy both in body and in spirit:*

> *but she that is married careth for the things of the world, how she may please her husband.*
>
>

1 Cor. 7:34

The purpose of this scripture is not to make Christians feel guilty about wanting to get married. It is merely saying that the single person has more time to devote to God's service with fewer distractions.

If you marry, ...or get remarried, you have not sinned. If you are single, you have done well. If you choose to remain single, it is because your spirit have gained power over your flesh. This also, is the favor of God. As a result of practicing, you have developed self-control over your body.

Although single, you have the responsibility of birthing spiritual babies into the Kingdom of God. You might also have the job of raising baby Christians to maturity in Christ.

A wife has the job of keeping her husband comfortable, and if he's the sole provider, then her job is shopping, cooking, cleaning, laundry, and helping the kids with their homework. She does this because she wants her husband to succeed in his work or ministry. God is in this, because He called them to work together on a ministry and family project.

Christians Should Not Impose
their Sexual Preferences Upon Others

If a person is content being single, he (or she) should not impose his (or her) views upon others. If others do not share in their contentment, or are uncomfortable with the idea of being single indefinitely, they should not be punished for their views. If they do get married (or remarried), it is the result of their faith in God.

Remarried People
Shouldn't be Put out of the Church

And the voice spake unto him again the second time,
What God hath cleansed, that call not thou common.
Acts 10:15

If Believers HAVE FAITH IN GOD TO PROVIDE THEM WITH A CHRISTIAN MATE, who are we to tell them, or God, "No!" If they have been loyal servants in the Kingdom of God, and just happened to fall in love, they shouldn't be punished. —If we really love people, we don't put them out of the church simply because they were blessed with someone special to spend the rest of their lives with!

There is nothing wrong with divorced Christians getting remarried, because God has washed them clean in His blood, and has forgiven their sins. There is nothing wrong when God blesses divorced Christians to share their lives with someone special. There is nothing wrong with having a happy marriage and enjoying a fulfilling sex life. And there's nothing wrong with having a beautiful family.

> ***...God has shown and taught me ...that I should not call any human being common ...or unclean.***

> *But in every nation he who ...has a reverential fear for God, treating Him with worshipful obedience and living uprightly,*

is acceptable to Him and sure of being received and welcomed [by Him].

Acts 10:28, 35 AMP

To Write, or For Book Orders

Divorce and Remarriage
$15 (includes taxes, and shipping and handling)
Send a Check or Money Order to:

Sims Publications Corporation
P.O. Box 300625
Jamaica, NY 11430-0625

1 (877) 219-8333

To Contact Author

Got Questions? sheilasims09@yahoo.com

For other books by Sheila Sims, visit my website: **sheilasimsbooks.com**

Thank You for helping to reach the world with the Gospel of Jesus Christ.

For live teachings, go to **sheilasimsbooks** *on Youtube.*

Lightning Source UK Ltd.
Milton Keynes UK
UKOW06f1357060715

254680UK00014B/517/P